# I AM THE FIRST

Success Secrets for First-time Entrepreneurs on
How to Navigate Entrepreneurship & Balance Life

# I AM THE FIRST

Success Secrets for First-time Entrepreneurs on How to Navigate Entrepreneurship & Balance Life

## Kevin R. McGee
## www.kevinRmcgee.com

Copyright © 2017 by Avid Entrepreneurship, LLC.

All rights reserved. No part of this publication may be reproduced, distributed, or transmitted in any form or by any means, including photocopying, recording, or other electronic or mechanical methods, without the prior written permission of the publisher, except in the case of brief quotations embodied in critical reviews and certain other noncommercial uses permitted by copyright law. For permission requests, write to the publisher, addressed "Attention: Permissions Coordinator," at the address below.

Avid Entrepreneurship
P.O. Box 170431
Atlanta, GA 30317

www.avidentrepreneursip.com
info@avidentrepreneurship.com
Ordering Information:
Quantity sales. Special discounts are available on quantity purchases by corporations, associations, and others. For details, contact Avid Entrepreneurship at the address above.

Printed in the United States of America

I Am the First: Success Secrets for First-time Entrepreneurs on How to Navigate Entrepreneurship & Balance Life.

ISBN 978-1545189191

1. Entrepreneurship   2. Success   3. Work Life Balance

# Contents

**Dedication**

**Acknowledgements**

**About the Book**

**About the Author**

**Chapter 1**                                 **21**
What Does It Take to Be the First Entrepreneur?

**Chapter 2**                                 **41**
The Real Deal on Entrepreneurship

**Chapter 3**                                 **53**
The Purpose of Entrepreneurship

**Chapter 4**                                 **65**
Strong Mind, Body and Spirit = Strong Business

**Chapter 5**                                 **77**
Balancing Family, Friends and Entrepreneurship?

**Chapter 6**                                 **93**
The Pros and Cons of Business Partnerships

**Chapter 7**                                 **107**
Nine Essential Mindsets for Entrepreneurial Success

**Chapter 8**                                 **115**
Failure is Feedback

**Chapter 9**                                 **125**
Taking the first steps towards starting your business

# Dedication

I would like to dedicate this book to my family both immediate and extended. Each of us exists not because of the choices that we have made, but rather because of the choices that our family before us made -- choices that allowed us to be birthed into this world. We continued to exist and grow because of the contributions of our family, be they immediate, extended or even adopted. Family is everything.

To my wife, Dionne, and my two daughters, Kayla and Amaya, I love you. Thank you for your patience and continuous love throughout this long continuous path less traveled that we continue to walk. We have not always had the finer things in life, but because of your love and support, things have always been fine.

We have endured many of the "joys" of entrepreneurship together. The highs and the lows. In the early years, there were seemingly more lows than highs. Thank you for your patience and for staying strong when our family endured skepticism, cynicism, financial loss, emotional stress and strain. If there is one thing that I regret about the entrepreneurial path that I have chosen, it would be the many missed opportunities to spend time with each of you.

The one thing that we never get more of or never replace is the time that we have lost. I pray every day that the choices that I make and time that I have missed from your lives are rewarded with a better more fulfilling life for all of us in the long run. Please know that everything that I have ever done and do in this vein, I do for you and our family generations in the future.

To my mother, Jacqueline McGee, and my father, Albert McGee, thank you both for staying actively engaged in my life. Over the years both of have been an indispensable source of knowledge, support, inspiration and motivation. Each of you has given me great and diverse perspective about the issues that I faced as a child and continue to face as a father myself.

I thank you both for investing time, money and effort into preparing me for the world I live in. Thank you both for exposing me to many firsts and affording me opportunities that were not always readily accessible.

Mom, we endured some lean years early in our journey. So, I thank you for your numerous sacrifices over the years as you raised a son while finishing college, going to law school, and becoming a state legislator all during a time when it was not a hospitable world for an African-American woman. Yet you continued to sacrifice your personal desires, needs and wants so that I could be better and do better. You have always made a point to expose me to opportunities that were not necessarily prescribed to be given to me as a young black man.

I have many memories of being a little boy, sitting in the back of the rooms of neighborhood meetings, college libraries and congressional offices while you worked and pursued your dreams. I didn't appreciate it much then, but the things that I heard and saw greatly influenced me. I thank you for sacrificing to send me to summer camps, educational events, and even trips across the world at a time when we could not afford it. You found a way. And thank you for being the first investor in my first businesses.

I hope that you know that every sacrifice you made for me was not in vain. By all reports, you have raised a son who has done well and has not had to sacrifice his character. Thus, it took a little longer to get where I was trying to be. I try every day to be a man that you can be proud of. You have always supported and encouraged my entrepreneurial dreams.

Dad, I thank you for your common sense and grounded advice over the years. You have been a good father and taught me a lot, even though much of what a father should know was not taught to you. As a father now, I understand how difficult a job it is, particularly with no role model. So, I thank you for modeling the aspects of what a father should be: loving, kind and compassionate. You have always been one to do for others, even when not doing for yourself.

You once told me years ago that I should "deal with people how they deal with me and not how they deal with other people. You never know why people treat other people the way that they do." This has been a key to my success in business and with people.

For me that meant that you give every person the benefit of the doubt until proven otherwise. It has helped me to not listen to the people who gossip and naysay about others. If I had listened to what other people said and went on their experiences with people rather than my own, I would have missed out on some great relationships and business opportunities. Thank you again for this nugget of wisdom.

Along with my parents are a host of family members who have all poured into me to make me the person that I am today. I can't name you all, but to my immediate aunts and uncles and my cousins, I say thank you.

Aunts: Pearl, Hazel, Gloria, Betty, and Teresa.
Uncles: Gus, George, Bobby, Sammy, Luther, James, and Earl Ricky.

To my siblings Erica, Tameisha, and Corey. Thank you for allowing me to be a part of your lives and for always sharing your perspective. Thank you for your confidence and trust in me as your "Big Brother." My conversations with you have always been very rewarding. Thank you.

And to the numerous extended aunts, uncles and cousins on both sides of my family, I sincerely thank you for the impact that you have had on my life. I fully realize that I exist and am the man that I am today because of all the interactions we have had since I was a child. We never know how the words and actions of others impact us. I thank you for every word and action, pleasant and unpleasant. They have all served me well and helped to define my character. I love and respect you all.

I would like to give a special thanks to my Uncle George, who gave me my first introduction to entrepreneurship. That experience left an indelible impression on me.

I have gained even more courage and strength from watching your journey over the years. You have tried many ventures and have experienced varied levels of success. But despite any losses, you have stuck with it. So please know that, for me, your biggest success has been serving as a mentor and stalwart example that you can live life on your own terms and create the life that you want through entrepreneurship. It may not always be the perfect life that many people strive for, but it is a life that belongs exclusively to you. And what can be more perfect than that?

# Acknowledgements

I would like to acknowledge A. Kenyatta Greer my friend, colleague, and editor. From the very beginning of my speaking and writing exploits, you have supported my efforts and used your talents as a wordsmith to help me express my sentiments on paper and in speech -- at times better than they were expressed in my thoughts. You have helped me truly understand the power that words, both written and spoken, have.

First and foremost, to the entrepreneurs of our past who embodied a great ideal of self-determination before a word was created to describe them. Much of what we taste, touch, feel, smell, and hear exists because someone had an idea, dream or vision and they followed through with it, despite the sacrifices it entailed.

For centuries, entrepreneurs have pushed through cynicism, skepticism and criticism to pursue that which was purposed in their hearts. They endured financial loss, social isolation, family ruin, and sometimes even loss of life, all to bring to market a product or service that they believed would make the world a better place. Through their successes and failures, they played their role and help inspire the continuum of entrepreneurship that exists today. They became the first, so they could ensure that they would not be the last.

To the thousands of entrepreneurs who I have had the pleasure to meet, instruct, coach or invest in, thank you. Over the past 25 years, I have learned so much from my interactions with you that has deeply impacted and enriched my life. Your stories have enabled me to add value to others embarking on the path of entrepreneurship by allowing me to share lessons learned, trials, tribulations and successes.

I would also like to acknowledge you, the aspiring or accomplished first-generation, first-time entrepreneur reading this book. You truly inspire me with your courage, tenacity, and faith in bringing to life that which has never been seen and that which hasn't existed. It is because of the dreams and ambitions of entrepreneurs like you that this country is great. I cannot begin to tell you the respect and admiration that I have for you and your undertaking.

You have taught me that entrepreneurship is more than starting a business. It is a strategy and way of thinking that allows you to live a life full of meaning and purpose. It is a hard journey that few dare to embark upon. But in the words of Robert Frost "Two roads diverged in a wood and I - I took the one less traveled by, and that has made all the difference." And a difference, indeed, you have and will continue to make with your entrepreneurial contributions to society.

## About the Book

This book, I Am the First, was written to primarily help first-generation, first-time entrepreneurs be more successful in the start-up of their small business. The title should recall the firsts that we have all had in our lives. But this entrepreneurial first is something special. Since it is targeted to the "firsts" it touches lightly on many subjects. This is intended to introduce the reader to certain concepts. More in-depth and subject-matter-specific writings are forthcoming.

For more than 25 years I have studied and engaged in entrepreneurial pursuits of all sorts. I have learned that entrepreneurship is more than simply starting a business. It is a way of thinking and acting that allows you to live a life full of meaning and purpose. I have truly seen the power of being the first entrepreneur in a family, a community or a group. It is transformative and creates opportunities and value for many people outside of the immediate sphere of influence of the entrepreneur.

This book is for those people who are on the cusp of entrepreneurship. For the people intrigued by the thought of running their own business, but not quite sure how to go about it. Or who are unsure of their ability to be successful at it. If you selected this book or began doing research, you are capable of doing it, and all you need is a little help and guidance. I want to help you, and I want this book to be a resource for you. One thing that I have learned about entrepreneurship and running businesses is that it is always, and I stress the word *always,* easier if you can learn from the mistakes of others. Learning from the successes of others is great, but learning from mistakes is even better.

This book and each chapter was written with both personal perspective and practical entrepreneurial insight. Each chapter has a standard structure. At the beginning, I cite a quote that captures the essence of the chapter. I then enlist the rule of three and give you the three key points that you should look for as you read the chapter. I call them the "Three Things To Think About." Then I conclude each chapter with a "Success Secret" that I hope will help you make wiser decisions.

Entrepreneurship is a journey and not a destination. Many people want to take the trip, but not many are willing to pay the price. This book purposely asks many open-ended questions. It is intended to challenge the readers to question themselves about why they are considering entrepreneurship and whether they are willing to take and complete this journey. As with any journey, the hardest part is often taking the first step. The Chinese philosopher Laozi has been credited with saying, "A journey of a thousand miles begins with a single step." That is so very true, and it is the reason that this book was written. It was written to help you take that first step and be more successful.

Success is really about the habits you have and how quickly you apply the lessons that you have learned from your experiences and observing the experiences of others. I have observed and interacted with some of the most successful and unsuccessful entrepreneurs in the world. I have seen multi-generational businesses, first-time family business, corporate entities, non-profits, partnerships and every imaginable business type and founder. I have talked with billionaire business owners and just-beyond-broke business owners and tried to determine what separates the two.

The deciding factor in the success of many the business that I have seen has not been access to capital or money, as many may believe. It has not been connections, as I take exception with "it's not what you know but who you know." Nor has it been the amount of education an individual has. More than anything, the deciding factor has been who or what you have been exposed to by way of entrepreneurship.

Meaning the most successful entrepreneurs have a wealth of entrepreneurial knowledge that they have gathered more by being mentored observers than by education. Whether they were mentored deliberately or not.

Success in business is not happenstance. It is the result of observing and learning from a well-defined network of relationships, practices, habits, and ideologies that help the entrepreneur deal with success *and* failure. And some degree of failure is all but inevitable in the life of any truly successful entrepreneur.

My hope is that this book helps to avert many of the potential failures and difficulties that starting a new business may bring to an individual. While you can never avoid all failure, removing many of the common reasons for failure will greatly improve your chances for success. I want to share what I have learned and what I have learned from others with you. Simply put, entrepreneurs learn more about successful entrepreneurship from other entrepreneurs than from anyone or anything else.

As I sat down to pen this book, I thought about how the information it contained would be different from the thousands of other entrepreneurship books that are on the shelves. I thought about the distinctive message I wanted to tell entrepreneurs. To that extent, this book focuses more on the humanistic aspects of entrepreneurship. It encourages the reader to fully balance his or her personal life and business. It encourages the reader to pursue entrepreneurship not for the sake of chasing money, but for the joy of chasing one's dreams and walking towards one's purpose.

In the face of this uncertainty, my keen entrepreneurial mind has few answers on how to solve or deal with this tragedy. Take away an entrepreneur's drive, determination and direction, and he or she is lost. But one thing that I have learned from entrepreneurship and life is that when you are lost, the best thing to do is to stop and return to what you know to be true. For me there is no truer thing or form of self-expression than entrepreneurship. As I thought deeper during this time, I was compelled to ask myself what more could I do to help others find this truth. How could I help others find this form of freedom and self-determination?

I Am the First is a must-read for aspiring and active entrepreneurs who need to be recharged, re-inspired or refocused to continue on the path of entrepreneurship. This book will help you look inside yourself, your business, and your family to be sure that you balance relationships for optimal success.

This book will not show you how to make a million dollars in the next six months. Nor will it show you how to make record profits without investing any money. But what it is guaranteed to do is to give you the strategies, tools, and techniques to increase your chances of success, thus enabling you and your family to live a long life of independence and freedom. You will gain insight and be inspired by the story of this entrepreneur and countless others who have made, and continue to make, the journey through entrepreneurship. Read these pages, apply the lessons, and increase your odds of success.

# About the Author

My journey in life has led me to be involved in endeavors as a serial entrepreneur, college trustee, executive chef, speaker, mentor, business coach, blogger and, recently, an advocate for pediatric cancer research. I am known for my candor and approachable demeanor -- both remnants of my humble upbringing in the rural Midwest. I continually try to connect with and inspire others.

For much of my life, I have been involved in some sort of entrepreneurial pursuit. As early as I can remember, I was selling candy and organizing my fellow five- and six-year-olds to do the same thing. I have tried to do just about everything. Much of it was, quite honestly, because I did not know any other way.

My first memory of entrepreneurship came from my Uncle George who owned a clothing store in Chicago. This was the big city compared to my modest Midwest home at the time. More importantly, this uncle gave all his nieces and nephews ten shares of stock in the menswear store. I remember how excited I was at the thought of owning something, even if I didn't know what a stock was. Living in such a poor community, I never really knew what it meant to own anything of value. That feeling of ownership was something that sticks with me even until this day.

Over the past two decades, I have started more businesses and had more ideas and aborted ventures than I care to remember. I have made a lot of mistakes and have had my share of misfortune when it comes to entrepreneurship. I have, at times, put my family through some difficulties as I pursued the things that I thought were best in terms of entrepreneurship. I have lost friends and acquaintances through failed business dealings. I have been sued and taken to court on a few occasions. My credit, at times, has suffered, and my spirit has been broken before.

But here's the thing: If I had the opportunity to choose my life path again, I would not have it any other way. There is something that is inherently good and satisfying for me about the spirit of entrepreneurship and the freedom that it brings. That freedom was put to the test in April 2015. On April 22, 2015, my oldest daughter, Kayla, was diagnosed with cancer, and my family's entire world was turned upside down. I looked back over my life and all that I had accomplished, as well as all that I still wanted to accomplish. And even with all that I had done, businesses that I had started, skills that I had acquired, I was, for all intents and purposes, lost for that moment in my life.

Because of this experience, I have learned that challenges and obstacles are not specific to a particular demographic. They affect us all indiscriminately. We can't control much of what happens to us, but we can control how we react and respond. I believe that we should respond by speaking life to our challenges and circumstances, always remembering to focus our voices and energies on those things that provide positive outcomes and feed the mind, body, and soul.

For me that thing is entrepreneurship. I have spent most of my life as an entrepreneur, starting my first venture at twenty-three years old. I have learned to recognize opportunities, overcome obstacles, deal with failures, and embrace success; these are lessons that I loves to share with others and lessons that I want to share with you.

Over the past twenty years, I have spoken to thousands of entrepreneurs and worked directly with hundreds of small businesses helping them to achieve their dreams and realize their goals. My early days were spent as an economic development and small business specialist in communities across the Southeast. Currently, through my company Avid Entrepreneurship, I provide small-business branding, consulting, and coaching. I have always been a constant and committed advocate for entrepreneurship and the study of entrepreneurs.

Through my thought leadership platform Speak Life, I deal with the universal themes of overcoming obstacles and pushing through failure, charging people with developing vision and direction as they learn to embrace success. This includes creating a space of genuine connectivity with others, a forum that allows participants to be vulnerable about their failures in order to promote positive change from within.

I have a true passion for entrepreneurship, and I believe that entrepreneurship is the only way to truly be in control of one's destiny. For those of us who have been marginalized by cultural biases and socioeconomic factors, entrepreneurship can be the great equalizer. No other activity has taken more families and individuals from poverty to prosperity like entrepreneurship has.

This book takes complex business principles like these and translates them into easy-to-understand concepts. I use real-life stories, analogies, and everyday examples to make this book a must read for those starting, or considering starting, a business.

20

# Chapter 1
## What does it take to be the first entrepreneur?

*"What this power is I cannot say; all I know is that it exists and it becomes available only when a man is in that state of mind in which he knows exactly what he wants and is fully determined not to quit until he finds it."*

*--Alexander Graham Bell*

## Three Things to Think About

1. Entrepreneurship is not just a whimsical notion. It takes a lot of hard work and determination.

2. It's not often that we must honestly assess and critique ourselves. But before starting a business you should honestly assess yourself. What are your strengths and weaknesses?

3. There are five questions every entrepreneur must be able to answer. They are the Who, What, When, Where and Why of entrepreneurship.

## What does it mean to say, "I Am the First?"

I am. Two of the most powerful words in the English language. Saying these two words immediately implies a certainty whether that be a perceived good or bad implication. For instance, I am successful or, conversely, I am not successful. Whatever you put after "I am" can greatly shape your situation or quite possibly your life.

But when you say, "I am" and you add the words "the first" the words take on an even greater meaning. To say I am the first immediately implies that you are experiencing or doing something that no one of your demographic has experienced or done before. The title of this book is intended to capture and emphasize that implication. When you are the first at entrepreneurship, or anything for that matter, you are navigating new territories. And often you are trying to do so with no map. You are felling your way as you go along. And that is very difficult to do.

When you make the decision to become an entrepreneur, that in and of itself is a huge undertaking. The rates for success at entrepreneurship and any level aren't that great. But when you go one step further and make the decision to become an entrepreneur and you will be the first to do so in your family, circle of influence, culture or community that is an even more massive undertaking.

But the most powerful thing about being the first entrepreneur, is that you in doing ensure that you will never be the last. You have set the standard and changed the narrative for all those around you. Even without knowing it, you are making an impact and being inspirational to generations to come. Many of them you may never know or see. That's the real power of successful entrepreneurship.

Being the first also implies a certain competitive nature among those who read this title from a different perspective. If there is a first, then there may be a last. This notion of competition is also implicit in the journey of entrepreneurship as well. Many entrepreneurs strive to be the best at what they do. They strive for the metaphorical "first place."

So, when you look at the power of being the first in entrepreneurship, you can see how this concept of setting the example is equally important in many other areas of life that may or may not include entrepreneurship. Whether you are the first man set foot on the moon, the first woman to run for President of the United States, the first child to escape a life of poverty, the first African-American to become President on the United States, the first Asian-American to be a member of Congress, or the first Hispanic-American to sit on the Supreme Court, being able to say that you are the first, in anything set's you apart from all others.

And each time that an individual becomes the first at something, they inspire their peers, to do the same and even better. Being the first creates a benchmark for others that sets the stage for friendly competition amongst one's own peers. The pride that we have when we see one of our peers achieve is sometimes short-lived when we say, if he/she did it, then I can do it to. This pride has now turned into confidence and a form of friendly competition.

I have always wondered why more of us don't positively compete against one another in our personal lives, jobs and careers and push one another to be more successful? Pushing to help one another become the respective "first," to accomplish things. It is simple in my mind, more of us should strive to be able to say the words "I am the first." And we should be able to say, "I Am the First" for many aspects of life.

I am the first to help fund cures for Cancer, I am the first to volunteer for to feed the homeless, I am the first to be a teacher in sub-Saharan Africa, I am the first to start a business, I am the first to not be incarcerated, I am the first to not die from heart disease, I am the first to stay married, I am the first to defeat alcoholism, and so on and so forth.

But as we know, there are not enough people who decide to take on this great burden of being the first. The reasons are varied but the main reason that people do not carry this burden is because it is a difficult thing to do. It is difficult to blaze a trail and get others to believe that this new way is the right way. In a world that seems to thrive and survive from conformity, there is little place for new ideas, diverse perspectives and unknown undertakings. In fact, much of our society ostracizes and isolates these "I Am the First" creative persons. The profit and praise don't come when the idea is first birthed in the mind of the creative, it only comes when the rest of the world catches on and decides that it is worthy of support.

Many people just can't deal with this level of criticism and skepticism. So, they continue to live their lives with very little divergence from their original path. Day in and day out. They do not seek to be the first, rather they seek to be the followers of the ones who blaze the trails.

But it is vital that more people strive to be the first, because the power of this feat inspires so many people in so many ways. The best example that I can think of is in the instance of runners. Up until 1954, it was not thought physically possible that the human body could run a mile in four (4) minutes. Scientists had long theorized and believed it to be a fact that the human anatomy could not handle the feat. It was believed that a runner's legs could not produce the power needed to run that fast and that their heart could not pump blood fast enough to supply the oxygen needed for the body.

But on May 6, 1954, Roger Bannister broke the 4-minute barrier, running the distance in 3:59.4. It has been stated that he credited his success to the practice of visualization, whereby he repeatedly pictured himself accomplishing this feat. After Roger's successful record-breaking run, several more runners in the coming years would run the mile in under four (4) minutes as well.

Today, it is very common for runners to accomplish this. In fact, since Roger broke the record more than 1,400 people have ran the mile in less than four (4) minutes. This is amazing since science, at the time, said it was impossible. But Roger believed otherwise and did not give up or quit until he defeated this goal and became the first to do so.

So, the real power in being the first and taking this step towards this entrepreneurial journey is that you will undoubtedly not be the last. Your courage, bravery, diligence, persistence and success will inspire countless others to run their own race and win.

## *What motivated me to become an entrepreneur?*

My first thoughts of becoming an entrepreneur started when I was around six years old. At the time, I did not even know how to spell the word entrepreneur, but I had gained an understanding of what it was. At the time, I was living in small poor rural town in Missouri. It was adjacent to an area known as the Mississippi Delta, then and now, one of the poorest regions in the nation.

I was a poor little black boy who had no knowledge of the world outside of this small town of 2,500 people. The town had one stop light, one grocery store, one high school, one major company that employed people and one railroad track that split the town in two and separated the white residents from the black residents. My parents both met there and were married very young. When I was 5-years old, they decided best if they separated and eventually they divorced.

I spent several years living with my grandmother who also lived in this small town. As a result, I had several aunts and uncles that would come through and visit my grandmother from time to time. I was an only child so I always loved when they visited and I received a break from the day-to-day routine. Many of them had lived in big cities and some had traveled around the world. Through their visits and stories, I would glean a glimpse of the outside world. The furthest that I had traveled at that time was St. Louis, Missouri.

I had one uncle in particular who lived in Chicago, my uncle George. On one of his trips to visit his mother, my grandmother, he informed me that he and some friends had started a haberdashery. Which he later informed me was a fancy word for a men's clothing store. He also told me that he had given all his nieces and nephews shares of stock in this new clothing enterprise.

I couldn't wait to tell my fellow 6-year old that I owned stock, even if I didn't know what it meant. I laugh to this day as I remember my excitement. But while I did not know what a stock was, I knew what it was to own something. I had never had that feeling before. But at that moment I knew what it felt like to own something of value. It was a feeling that has never left me. And one that I always strived for.

In the coming summers, I would travel to Chicago and visit this haberdashery to check on my investment. As I walked through the store and saw the merchandise, inventory and employees, I was fascinated. Listening to my uncle and his partners give instructions to the employees and discuss the affairs of the business was intriguing. I was hooked. I had to be the person in charge going forward.

When I returned to my hometown, I now looked at my surroundings with new perspectives. In my meager surroundings, no one owned anything of real value. This was a very poor town and there were few businesses. So, there were few jobs and opportunities to work. And for the businesses that did exist, neither my family or I had access to be a part of them or be employed by them. All we could do was patronize these businesses and be consumers. We had no opportunity to enjoy the benefits of business ownership.

But now, through my uncle's business, I felt that I owned a part of an enterprise that was hundreds of miles away in the big city. For a moment in my mind, I could leave the small town and travel to my business in a far-away place. That feeling of ownership is one that has always stuck with me to this day and is the reason that I have pursued entrepreneurship. There is something about owning a business, that for me, gives meaning to life that you live and the contributions that you make.

Through entrepreneurship and business ownership you become a contributor rather than merely a consumer. I have always wanted to be a person that added value to whatever I was involved in or a part of. So, for me this first ownership experience lit the spark that would eventually start the fire and fuel my passion for entrepreneurship.

I share that story to show you what motivated and continues to motivate me. But the question I would like to ask you is, what is motivating you to start your own business?

### *What is motivating you to become an entrepreneur?*
You have read my story of entrepreneurial motivation, so what's yours? Do you know or have you thought about why you want to become an entrepreneur? Are you motivated by a lifelong dream, career ambition, desire for financial security, or do you want to add something of value to the world?

Whatever the reason, you must think deeply about what it is that is motivating you to take this journey.

### *Are you qualified for entrepreneurship?*
I don't believe that anyone would question the assertion that you need a specific skill set and personality to be an entrepreneur. Without a doubt, many will openly tell you that they do not have the

fortitude to be an entrepreneur. In my experience, I can recount several stories where people question why a person would choose entrepreneurship. I remember one person in particular who said "I could never do what you do. Starting a business and not knowing where your check was coming from would scare me to death."

There are also countless numbers of stories where individuals have started small businesses only to find out after a short time that they had no desire to be in business for themselves. And there are even more stories of individuals who have started small businesses that have been unsuccessful, but who continue to pursue the seemingly elusive success and never give-up. So, what is it that determines whether an individual decides to pursue his/her entrepreneurial endeavors no matter what or decides to quit at the first encounter with failure?

There is some discussion on whether entrepreneurs are born or made. There is no persuasive evidence that points to either perspective. But if I had to rely on my own experience, I would say that entrepreneurs are born. Within all the successful entrepreneurs that I have met, counseled, consulted with and coached, there were some innate traits and characteristics akin to instinct.

These same traits are not present in everyone. I have met many people who work in the corporate sector who have no intention or desire to ever work for themselves. And they choose to do so not because they lack entrepreneurial ability or financial resources; it is that they simply have no desire to do so. Many people are happy and fulfilled with their careers and will likely never pursue entrepreneurship.

But real entrepreneurs are not happy unless they are engaged in some aspect of active entrepreneurship. It is not enough for them to exist in environments with high-levels of intellectual capacity and abundant financial resources. They must constantly feed the flames of the entrepreneurial dreams that burn in their hearts. Entrepreneurs pursue business ownership and self-determination at all costs. Not only in the United States, but all over the world.

In other parts of the world, entrepreneurs exist and thrive as well. Many of them have no college degrees, MBA's or formal education. Many of them are poor and come from challenged backgrounds. They are entrepreneurs often out of necessity and don't have to ask the question, "are they qualified?" Clearly this indicates that entrepreneurship, and one's choice to pursue it, are not dependent solely on intellectual capacity, financial resources, or a solid business acumen. But all of the aforementioned become necessary at some point. But you have a choice and you have many more resources at your disposal. So, take advantage of the opportunity to make an informed decision about your entrepreneurial journey.

Every day thousands of individuals decide to take a step towards entrepreneurship. According to the Small Business Administration, more than 17,000 business start each day. That's more than 6 million businesses that are started every year. An even larger number though tend to close each year. Many of these start-ups are new first-time entrepreneurs who have decided to take the entrepreneurial journey.

What is it that makes them decide to take this leap? What is it within them that makes them feel that they would be successful in entrepreneurship? Everyone who starts a business believes that they will be successful. Surely no one would become an entrepreneur with the intention of failing. So, what is it that these brave souls see either in themselves or in the market that makes them move towards entrepreneurship.

One of the key tenets of successful entrepreneurship is the ability to perceive opportunities where others do not. In academia, this process is known as cognition, which essentially means one's ability to understand and recognize opportunities. But to perceive and recognize an opportunity is not enough. To become an entrepreneur, you must also identify a way that you can exploit this opportunity and create a viable business model. This is loosely referred to as ideation, or more simply the process of vetting ideas for your business. Sadly, many entrepreneurs get to this stage and stop.

Hopefully your purchase of this books means that you want to do more than have a great idea. So, what is your idea? What problem does it solve or what need does it meet? There can be no business, and there can be no success, if the idea that you are contemplating does not solve a problem or meet an essential need. Does your idea meet these criteria? Do you think that you have the fortitude to take your idea to the next level?

Entrepreneurs also often possess innate traits such as extroversion and a propensity for risk-taking. But this propensity does not mean that they take risks carelessly. Quite the opposite. Many successful entrepreneurs careful vet endeavors before making the decision to start a business or venture.

## *Walking the road less traveled*

When you talk about becoming an entrepreneur, you are talking about embarking on a journey that few people have successfully navigated. It is without a doubt walking the road that is less traveled. As a matter of fact, only a small fraction of people have the courage, conviction, and resolve to even consider entrepreneurship. If we did the numbers, it would tell us that less than 2% of the U.S. population embark upon entrepreneurship annually. And if you are a first-generation entrepreneur and the first person in your family to engage in entrepreneurship, you are going down a new path. Walking the road less traveled means that you will cover new territory and new ground that is not been covered before. This means that you will have to do things that you've never done before, including things that are, perhaps, somewhat out of your comfort zone.

This journey is also one that you may have to initially take alone. Chances are that you will not have a lot of support and encouragement when you begin. As mentioned earlier, entrepreneurship is still something that is foreign to many people. The road is less traveled for a reason, it is difficult. Most living and even non-living things are programmed to pursue the path of least resistance. If you have ever toyed with an insect walking on the ground, simply put something in front of it and it will go another way. Unfortunately, people are not very different.

Put another way, most people do what is easiest and causes the least amount of stress. Even water flows around obstacles to a path of least resistance. It flows downstream and not upstream. But as an entrepreneur, you will often be pushing upstream against the current and momentum of everything else. And it is this tension created by pushing against the norm that causes the entrepreneurial ingenuity that we have heard of with many great entrepreneurs. Vanguard entrepreneurs like Henry Ford, Madame C.J. Walker, Bill Gates, Steve Jobs and many others have pushed against the current and created things that were very foreign during the times that they started their ventures.

As an entrepreneur, you have a choice when you encounter obstacles in your journey. You can stop and turn around, go around, go over, or go through. The choice is yours to make. But if you do not make a choice, life will make one for you. Entrepreneurs very rarely back down or turn around when they are faced with a challenge. They may pivot or take a different path, but they always try to continue the journey and push through obstacles. If this is something that you instinctively do, then maybe entrepreneurship is for you.

## *Acknowledging your inner entrepreneur*

Does "Acknowledging your inner entrepreneur" sound like some religious experiential task? Perhaps it sounds like the first part of some twelve-step anti-addiction program. If you are going to be an entrepreneur, you must first acknowledge who and what you are. You are different than many others in your circle. A key part of being an entrepreneur is to recognize and acknowledge that you are different than most people. The fact that you are considering entrepreneurship indicates a few key things. It means that you have made the determination that you want to live a different type of life. It means that you have decided that you want to be in control of not only your daily life but also your ultimate destiny. There is something inside of you that you want to share with the world.

If you are a true entrepreneur, no matter what the situation, you will always see the potential in every opportunity and challenge. The challenge is determining if the idea is feasible and if it realistically has the potential for profit. Do you get excited by thoughts of the next big thing? Well, you are not crazy, or childish, or immature or any of the other things that the naysayers call you.

**Ask yourself:**
When I'm going about my daily tasks, do I find myself constantly thinking that there must be a better way?

Do I think about ways to make life easier or safer for others?

Do you find yourself dreaming of living a life of freedom and flexibility?

Do you feel sometimes like you are the odd person when you are surrounded by your friends and colleagues?

If you answered yes to several of these questions then you likely have that entrepreneurial spirit. But having an entrepreneurial spirit, great ideas and dreams is not enough. Your innate skill and entrepreneurial instincts must be honed and sharpened just like any other God-given ability. And I do believe that the ability to start businesses and create is a gift from God. And if by chance you don't believe in God, after you have attempted to start enough businesses, you will.

Much of the population will never have the exceptional ideas and instinctual insight that you do about business and life. Life for most people is a series of 9-to-5 routines that make them believe that they are secure. Many people could sit around all day and not have one idea pop into their heads. That's the tragedy of it all. Unfortunately, many would be entrepreneurs are surrounded by these types of people who do not strive for more. For many of them, mediocrity works.

It is hard to be surrounded by people who all have a mindset and you are the exception. But you should remember that being the exception is a precursor for being exceptional. I would suspect that for most of your life your family, friends, and coworkers have been saying some things about you. Some have said that you have a great business mind and should start your own business, others have called you unrealistic, daydreamer, fairytale chaser, etc. And still others have thought that you have wasted time as you have pursued your dreams. I have two things to say to that; follow your instincts and find other, positive people to be around. You are not a dreamer or a fairytale chaser. You are not unrealistic. And you are not wasting your time. You are an entrepreneur – plain and simple – and, unfortunately, there are not a lot of people willing to do what you do, so you find yourself feeling somewhat alone.

You have decided to live you're a life a few years like most people won't, so you can spend the rest of your life like most people can't.

And in the case of families like the Ford's, Gates' or others, you will live like most people can't for multiple generations. In fact, acknowledging the fact that you want to be an entrepreneur, in this author's mind, is accepting a calling, not unlike a doctor, lawyer, pastor or priest does.

In acknowledging that you want to become an entrepreneur, you are acknowledging several things. One is that you want to be in control of your destiny. Another is that you may want to employ others and offer them an opportunity to provide for them and their family. Or perhaps you want to bring your invention to the market and change the world. Whether you want to empower your local community by starting a neighborhood business or impact the world, entrepreneurship can make your dream possible. As you acknowledge your passion for entrepreneurship, it is equally important that you consider to what extent you want to go.

Also, inherent in the process of acknowledging your inner entrepreneur is considering the next steps that you must take to move closer to your goal. Acknowledgment and subsequent action should go hand-in-hand.

## *Assessing yourself for entrepreneurship*

Equally important as acknowledging your inner entrepreneur is that you also do a quick assessment of yourself and your business ideas. This will help you better determine who you are and what it is that you want to do. There is a simple process that I advise my clients to use to do this. It includes an age-old method that I refer to as the 5Ws of entrepreneurship. The who, what, when, where, and why of yourself and your business idea.

## *Who are you?*

On the surface, this is a seemingly easy question to answer. If I were to ask you this question in person, you would respond with your name, what you do for a living, and, possibly, where you're from. You may also give me some general information about your background and work history. But the question that you need to ask yourself is who are you in relation to the world in the business you have started or propose to start. So, for instance, if you had started an educational consulting firm, you may answer the question as follows: "My name is John, and I am an entrepreneur who believes in the ability of education to empower and uplift. I am a person who believes that everyone deserves an opportunity to be educated in this country. I am also a mentor and teacher and have devoted a large portion of my life to helping young people overcome educational challenges." Do you see the difference?

If you are serious about entrepreneurship there should be some higher sense of purpose in what you want to do. For years I owned and operated restaurants. Many of my friends and family thought that I did this because I loved food. While I do love food, the reason that I started businesses in this tough industry is because I have a fundamental belief that everyone should eat good things. Coming from a poor upbringing, eating a great meal was a rare luxury for me. So, when I started my hospitality endeavors, it was with this internal purpose that I fueled my passion.

Anything that you do in life that will require as much time and demand as much of you as entrepreneurship does, must have deep purpose. As you start your venture, who you are will be of great importance. As your business grows, you will encounter challenges and obstacles, as well as opportunities. It will be essential that you remember who you are and what you stand for. Remembering who you are will help you to maintain focus, stay the course, and remain true to your mission. Asking the question of who you are also helps you to define the next question: what.

### *What is it that you want to share with the world?*
Most entrepreneurs don't necessarily think about their business in terms of what they are sharing with the world; but, in actuality, the very essence of entrepreneurship, bringing a product or service to market, is when you have identified that there is something you think the marketplace is missing and made the determination that you want to provide it. There is a problem that you wish to solve. There is value that you want to add.

You would be surprised at the value even small things add to the world. There is an entrepreneur named Lonnie Johnson from Mobile, Alabama. **Lonnie** is an African American inventor and engineer who holds more than 80 patents. He is best known for the Super Soaker water gun, which has ranked among the world's top 20 best-selling toys every year since its release. A water gun may not seem like something that could change the world. But think of how many happy children, and adults, that this invention has created around the world. Can you put a price on the value of more happiness in the world? Imagine how many smiles this invention has created. How many family outings have been made more fun? How much is happiness worth? So, no matter what your idea is, it has the potential to make a difference. He has made millions of dollars, but more importantly he has created hundreds of millions of smiles.

### *When did you decide that you wanted to be an entrepreneur?*
As you recount the stories of successful entrepreneurs, they all tend to have a story of when they first got the idea to start their business. Earlier I told you my *when*. It was when I was six-years-old and my uncle gave me stock. Often, people decide to become entrepreneurs because of an internal need or desire like mine. Or perhaps it was started because of some traumatic event, like the loss of a loved one

that inspired someone to create an invention or therapy. Or a loss on a child due to an accident that inspired a person to create a safety device. You should know *when* you made that decision to become an entrepreneur. The *when* is so important because it can always serve as your north star when things get sketchy.

### *Where do you want to make an impact?*
Deciding where you want to make an impact is important. As a start-up entrepreneur, chances are your resources will be limited, so it is important that you identify where you want to make an impact. It will be difficult to impact everywhere and everyone immediately. Ask yourself what *type* of impact you want to make with your business. Local? Neighborhood or community impact? Or do you want to make an impact in your state or perhaps even across the nation? Whatever your answer, it will, to a great degree, determine the type of business you establish and how you market and grow your business. It will also help you determine the types of resources (both human and financial) you'll need to make the type of impact you desire.

The question of where also pertains to where you physically, or even virtually want to start your business. Where you want to impact will influence where your business is located. For instance, if you want to impact children on the Southside of town and you locate your business on the Northside of town, you may not be positioned to make that business a success. Or if you want to have an online business, but you spend most of your time creating one-on-one in person relationships and less time building out your online platform. Where matters a great deal. As the saying goes "location is everything".

### *Why do you want to become an entrepreneur?*
Perhaps the most important question is "*why?*". Why would you want to become an entrepreneur and subject yourself to all the trials that are incumbent with entrepreneurship? If your desire to become an entrepreneur is so that you will have more money, I must inform you

that while entrepreneurship is a way to obtain financial security, it is not necessarily the easiest.

If you want to become an entrepreneur so that you will have more time to spend with your friends and family, I must inform you again that entrepreneurship often means that you spend more time working in your business than you would working a nine-to-five job. But it is the long-term goal of financial freedom and increased family time that are the pay-offs.

Why is also important because there will undoubtedly be times when you are questioning why you made this choice. When you are stressed and strained, when your resources are low, and things seem a little dim, you must be able and look yourself in the mirror and tell yourself why you are doing this. Why is perhaps the most important question that you have to ask yourself.

So, whatever your reason, identify it from the beginning, because when times get tight, and challenges and obstacles arise, the *who*, *what*, *when*, *where*, and *why* will keep you motivated and moving forward.

## ✹ Success Secrets

One of the secrets of success in entrepreneurship is having a sound understanding of who you are, what you are capable of and what type of value that you want to add to the world. The burden of becoming the first to do anything is extremely heavy. But the short and long-term rewards outweigh the burden.

You should know and believe that in your acceptance of shouldering this burden there is an implicit higher calling and meaning to your actions. You are doing more than deciding to do something. You are making a statement that because of your actions some small or large part of the world will be changed for the better.

Many have mistaken a great idea as a call to start a business. The great idea is only a small portion of starting a business. In fact, the idea or concept is the easy part. Putting all the other essential small-business methodologies in place is what stops many people. Entrepreneurship is not an easy notion, and it's not for the fainthearted. It is a way of life, and you have to be ready for it. Before you step out, make sure that you are ready!

# Chapter 2

## The Real Deal on Entrepreneurship

*"Entrepreneurship is living a few years of your life like many people won't, so that you can spend the rest of your life like most people can't".*

*-Unknown*

### Three Things to Think About

1. Entrepreneurship is more than just having a great idea and starting up. There is a science behind it.

2. There will always be more failures than successes in entrepreneurship, the numbers prove that. So, you should educate yourself on the business of entrepreneurship to improve your chances of success.

3. People start businesses for many different reasons. You should decide, before you start your business, what type of entrepreneur you want to be.

## *The history of entrepreneurship*

It's hard to imagine, but once upon a time, long, long ago, everyone was an entrepreneur of sorts. Before communities and kingdoms were organized, everyone and every family created some sort of good or performed some sort of service. These goods and services were used for the betterment of the communities. Many people bartered their goods and services for commensurate goods and services of others. Commerce was a regular part of daily life and everyone had to produce and or create something in order to survive.

There were no organized enterprises during the early ages, and creativity was all that allowed people to live and thrive. In this environment, the idea of entrepreneurship created a mutual dependency for individuals and communities. Maybe things should be that way still. As times advanced, nations were dependent upon one another for the goods and services that they respectively produced. No one nation or person could produce everything that they needed to survive. And so it still is today. No one person or nation can produce everything that it needs to remain viable.

As the world grew and commerce became more complex, entrepreneurs became a more integral part of society – although not as highly regarded as the people they often served. Think back to the earliest possible times that you have learned of, and you will find entrepreneurs there. Then, we simply called them blacksmiths, merchants, lodge owners, farmers, carpenters, etc.

It is believed that the term "entrepreneur" did not come about until the nineteenth century. It was a loanword from French and was first used in the early 1700s. Jean-Baptiste Say, a French economist, is believed to have coined the word. He defined an entrepreneur as "one who undertakes an enterprise, especially a contractor, acting as intermediary between capital and labor." Today, the term entrepreneur is applied to a person who is willing to help launch a new venture or enterprise and accept full responsibility for the outcome.

In all the aforementioned definitions, entrepreneurship focuses on a person's desire to engage in commerce and assume the risk or reward. In the early days, failure at entrepreneurship could have meant death. Make a bad sword for the king, and end up on the chopping block. Those are pretty high stakes.

From these humble beginnings, we in the United States have made a correlation between entrepreneurship, the attainment of wealth and prosperity, and intelligence. We have elevated entrepreneurs and believe that wealth is a key tenet of entrepreneurship. But there is nothing in any definition that I have seen that would suggest any such true correlation."

Today entrepreneurship and what constitutes an entrepreneur has grown greatly. With the invention and application of the internet, there is virtually an infinite number of business possibilities. In early times, the number of viable business models was limited. But today the sky is the limit in terms of the types of businesses and entrepreneurs there are.

## The business of entrepreneurship

While entrepreneurship is about pursuing your dreams and your passions, there is some science behind it. And make no mistake, entrepreneurship is also about business.

According to the SBA, small businesses have from one to 499 employees, and their revenues generally do not to exceed $35 million dollars. That's a huge range, and it varies even more by industry.

As of 2013, there were 28,443,856 small businesses; 5,707,941 small businesses with employees; 22,735,915 small businesses without employees (non-employers); and 56,062,893 workers employed by small businesses.

The highest number of small businesses were in California (3,622,304), Texas (2,412,717), Florida (2,180,556), New York (2,057,959), Illinois (1,169,961), Pennsylvania (999,591), Georgia (962,085), Ohio (926,977), Michigan (856,682), and North Carolina (833,107).

Based on current statistics, only 61% of these businesses will exist five years after starting, and only 33% will exist for more than ten years. Not the best odds in the world. But what do odds mean to an entrepreneur?

Consistently, small businesses with one to 499 employees continue to add more net new jobs than large businesses (500+ employees). Companies with one to 49 employees have typically contributed the most to job growth. I offer an example. Imagine if a Fortune 500 company and a small business with two employees both received a million-dollar grant. For the large corporation, one million dollars might be a fraction of its daily overhead. For a small mom-and-pop organization, the same one million dollars would immediately go back into the economy. The small business would hire more employees, secure more space, buy more raw materials, and do more advertising. Small businesses immediately inject money into the economy.

But what we are really talking about as it relates to you is microbusinesses, more commonly called mom-and-pop shops. Microbusinesses are defined by the SBA as firms with one to nine employees. They are, by far, the most common kind of employer. According to the SBA, America's 3.7 million microbusinesses made up 75.3 percent of all private-sector employers in 2013, and they provided 10.8 percent of the private-sector jobs (Source: Bureau of Labor Statistics, Business Employment Dynamics). Most microbusinesses are more than five years old. But do not be dismayed. Practically every Fortune 500 company started as a small mom-and-pop shop.

The fact of the matter is that now, more than ever, there are an infinite number of ways to become an entrepreneur. With technology, you don't even have to leave your home to do it.

## *Types of entrepreneurs and their motivations*

<u>Capitalistic entrepreneurs</u>
Capitalistic entrepreneurs are probably what most people think about when they think about traditional entrepreneurs and entrepreneurship. A capitalistic entrepreneur is one who goes into business for one purpose and one purpose only: to make money, as much money as possible. For many capitalistic entrepreneurs, personal passion is not a necessity. These types of entrepreneurs rely more heavily on making data-driven decisions of risk versus return. Their only concern is that the numbers make sense. This is reminiscent of the 2000s television series "Shark Tank."

These entrepreneurs generally have little concern about the social impact of their ventures. Nor do they have a great degree of concern for the environmental impact of their ventures. Their only concern is to make as much as they possibly can while investing as little as they possibly can.

Many of the comforts we enjoy today are the result of the profit-driven mindset of capitalistic entrepreneurs. These entrepreneurs did not desire to have a social impact when they were starting their businesses, but there are numerous instances of the descendants of capitalistic entrepreneurs taking the wealth that was amassed and putting it to use serving the public good.

Social Entrepreneurs
The term "social entrepreneur" is relatively new. In essence, it describes an entrepreneur who does not necessarily have a purely capitalistic interest in starting a business. Rather, a social entrepreneur is motivated almost exclusively by his or her desire to help, improve, and impact society in a positive manner. In former years, the business a social entrepreneur starts might simply have been called a non-profit organization. Today, though, the perception of non-profits is less than glamorous. While the positive attributes are a non-profit's ability to help others or address a social need, the negative connotations of a non-profit with regard to the business world are more common.

Now, when people think of non-profit organizations, they tend to think of inefficiency, lack of structure, lack of business acumen, and lack of sustainability. The term "social entrepreneurship" is a purposeful attempt to combine both the capitalistic meaning of entrepreneurship and the social emphasis of a non-profit. This new term places more of an emphasis on the founder's desire to impact society while creating a sustainable organization that an entrepreneur would follow. It is the best of both worlds.

Many organizations started by social entrepreneurs do not have an official non-profit tax status like traditional non-profit organizations do. Rather, they use a business model that puts an emphasis on efficiently operating a business to create a profit and then reinvesting or directing that profit directly towards the social cause that is advocated by the founder(s). A social entrepreneur can start a company that is for profit or not for profit. There is no limitation to the type of business that he or she can establish. The only hallmark is that the founder is driven primarily by an intrinsic desire to help others.

Often, the social entrepreneurial ventures transcend continental boundaries and extend their focus to alleviating social ills around the world. Social entrepreneurs tend to do a good job of employing technology to address issues in areas of the world that largely lack access to technology. They employ different types of Web-based platforms to connect the global recipients of their generosity to the individual funders. For example, there is a social entrepreneurial organization called Kiva that provides small loans to entrepreneurs around the world. In emerging countries in the East, they provide small-dollar loans to villagers to create businesses.

In the United States, they provide large or small business loans to entrepreneurs to start their businesses. They do this by employing a Web-based application that allows individual citizens like you and I to electronically contribute small amounts of money to a fund that Kiva then administers largely through intermediaries who use similar electronic technology. So here you have a highly technology-driven solution to provide something as simple as seeds to a small farmer in Africa who has never even used the Internet. In essence, the social entrepreneurs are adept at providing complex yet simple solutions for simple problems, which seems almost paradoxical.

Serial Entrepreneurs
Serial entrepreneurs are pretty much exactly what the name implies. These are individuals who have repeatedly started businesses that may or may not have been successful. Serial entrepreneurs are also gluttons for punishment. The ultimate goal of serial entrepreneurs is to determine the basic tenets of entrepreneurial success. This is not to say that everything that they try will be successful, but rather that they have created or discovered a methodology for starting businesses that have an increased chance of success.

Lifestyle Entrepreneurs

Another type of entrepreneurship that is gaining in popularity is lifestyle entrepreneurship. A lifestyle entrepreneur places personal lifestyle and passion before profit. This entrepreneur has decided to combine business with personal interest, talents, and abilities to create an entity that allows him or her self-expression while also creating additional time to spend with friends and family, or doing enjoyable things. Slightly different than a social entrepreneur, lifestyle entrepreneurs do not necessarily engage in businesses that have a social accountability component. Instead they engage in the business of their choice if they give them the flexibility and freedom that they desire.

Often, for lifestyle entrepreneurs, making money is secondary to preserving their lifestyles. In recent years, this type of entrepreneurship has become particularly popular with stay-at-home parents. The desire to be an impactful force in the household has overridden the desire to be able to afford all the luxuries of life. As families become more educated, both spouses have their own personal interests. Lifestyle entrepreneurship has allowed many to stay at home while also building a business and doing what they love. Lifestyle entrepreneurs are often more successful when they have a counterpart or spouse that is charged with the primary responsibility of supporting the household.

**First-generation entrepreneurship**

Many of the people who read this book will be first-generation entrepreneurs. You will be the first in your immediate family to try your hand at starting a business. It is important that you understand what it means to be a first-generation entrepreneur. There can be a steep learning curve for first-timers. Success for this group is not even remotely guaranteed. But there are some things that you should consider as you take this leap.

In business, success – particularly financial solvency – is dependent upon many variables. More so than education and knowledge,' there are several other factors that play a part in the success of many of America's most successful companies, both large and small. Being successful does not mean that one entrepreneur is smarter or better than anyone else. Often, it means that entrepreneur had a different set of relationships and experiences that positioned him or her for success. These experiences can include purposeful steps one takes, like going to specific colleges or engaging in specific classes. It could mean self-education, too. Largely, though, it is a matter of opportunity: being in the right place at the right time with the right product.

Consider family history, if you will. A close examination of many successful entrepreneurs will show that, more often than not, they had a family history of entrepreneurship and small-business ownership. This is an invaluable aspect of entrepreneurial success since, as they say, experience is the best teacher. Being able to draw upon the experience of your family is a great benefit. Also, the wealth that has been generated through family businesses serves as a great buffer against failure. While money isn't everything, it does have the ability to mitigate business mistakes.

As a culture, we have somehow diminished the value in providing a good, simple life for our families. As a result, many first-generation entrepreneurs go into business with visions of being a millionaire in a few short years. Entrepreneurs who start businesses exclusively for monetary reasons may find themselves disappointed or embarrassed if their enterprises do not make the type of revenue that people perceive it should. For instance, if your business is making $250,000 a year, that does not mean that you are making $250,000 a year. There is gross revenue and net revenue. As an entrepreneur, you only get net revenue. You may be the last to get paid if you have vendors, landlords, and employees.

But, entrepreneurship can be financially lucrative. It just takes time. It does not happen overnight. It's almost never the romanticized rags-to-riches stories we hear about on television. For instance, what about the rags-to-riches story of Donald Trump, a multi-millionaire and one of the most well-known and well oft-mentioned entrepreneurs. His television shows and other marketing tactics provide an image of a self-made man who pulled himself up by his boot straps and built a dynasty. Upon closer review, though, you'll find that The Donald's road to success was somewhat paved by his family. Donald Trump's father was a rich man. And Donald Trump's grandfather was a rich man, too. Donald Trump's grandfather was an immigrant who created wealth for his family by investing in real estate.

Fred Trump, Donald's father, received a hefty inheritance when Donald's grandfather died. Through savvy business deals, also in real estate, he turned this into a fortune of over $200 million in the 1960s – a sum that would equate to $billions today. So, not only did Donald have access to real estate know-how, but he also had millions with which to work. He did not stray far outside of his comfort zone, focusing much of his activities on real estate. Now, this is not intended to take anything away from the accomplishments of Donald Trump or his father Fred Trump. They are indeed great businessmen. There are many heirs to family inheritances that simply sat on their butts and spent all the inheritance partying and engaging in excess, ending up squandering the family fortune. The point here is that the likelihood of striking it rich right away are slim. Take some time to understand how successful entrepreneurs became successful.

## ☼ Success Secrets

The beauty of entrepreneurship is that there are no predetermined rules regarding what type of business you will start. That is also the obstacle. There is no magic formula for success. Only habits, principles, and behaviors that you can follow.

Many people romanticize becoming an entrepreneur; but when you really look at the numbers, the odds are drastically against you. Do your research, and make sure that you separate the fact from the fiction. Be prepared to invest the time and resources that you need to become successful. Entrepreneurship is a long-term game.

# Chapter 3

## The Purpose of Entrepreneurship

*"Every man or woman is born into this world to do something unique and distinctive, and if he or she does not do it, it will not be done."*

*- Benjamin E. Mays*

### Three Things to Think About

1. Purpose is an often-overlooked aspect of entrepreneurship. But having purpose in what you do is important.

2. You should consider your reason to pursue entrepreneurship carefully. Your entrepreneurial purpose may be to find a way to use your past and your experiences to improve the lives of others.

3. The common thread through all the reasons and purposes of entrepreneurship is to help create more freedom of some kind. The freedom to do the things you desire, the freedom to express your creativity or the freedom to help others.

## *Reasons to take the entrepreneurial journey*

If you are reading this book, you are considering entrepreneurship and its benefits. Do you know what caused you to want to start a business? In my experience, I have found that there are two main reasons that people decide to become entrepreneurs. The number one reason is freedom. Be that financial, career or lifestyle freedom. The number two reason is altruism. People want to be able to contribute to the local, national or even global community. For entrepreneurs, the only way to achieve true freedom and happiness is by controlling their own careers and professional destinies. Entrepreneurs must own something and be in control of some aspect of their lives.

Are you in control of your career at the moment? Are reading this book at work, when you should be working? Are you reading this book on your lunch break? Perhaps you are reading it during one of the approved fifteen-minute breaks you are allowed by law per day. Or perhaps you are reading it prior to going to bed and must stop at some point because you have to get up at six o'clock tomorrow morning to get ready for work.

Does your current job provide you with all the money that you need to live the type of life that you want to live? Or better yet are you working multiple jobs to make the ends meet? Money is in no way the answer to all our problems, but it does make many problems more manageable.

How many people do you know who absolutely love their job? How many people do you know who wake up early, excited about going to work every day? Is that you? How many people would stay at their current job and work for free if money were no issue? More than likely you do not know very many people who could answer yes to the questions above.

The reality is that there are few people who really love their jobs and would work for free – and who would even work forever. But by the same token how many companies truly love the people that work for them? Do you think the people who worked for large companies during the 2008 recession felt that their companies had their best interests at heart? Does anyone remember Enron? The days of big pensions and hefty retirements are gone. What is the reward today for working for a company for all your life? Not much.

Maybe working for a company for thirty years and ending up with absolutely nothing to show for it sounds good to you, but I doubt it. While I am not suggesting that entrepreneurship is the answer to all your career problems, or that it is a silver bullet to a problem-less life. I am saying that of all the options that exist to improve the quality of life for you and your family, I believe that entrepreneurship ranks at the top. Let me rephrase that, successful entrepreneurship ranks at the top. Entrepreneurship can provide a good life for you and your family. It can give you the finances, freedom, and flexibility to live the type of life that you should enjoy.

So, if you currently have a job but you feel that entrepreneurial urge poking you in the stomach, see which category you fall into below.

**These are the ten most common complaints from workers that I have polled over the past twenty years as they relate to working at their jobs.**

**1. Your pay is too low.** I bet you could have guessed that one. Did you happen to get your $1.2 million-dollar bonus last year? Even though the company lost money?

**2. You make less than a less-skilled coworker.** Why *should* you both get the same pay? After all, Bill has known the boss for much longer than you have. Never mind you do more work than he does.

**3. Mediocre healthcare benefits.** Hooray for free healthcare! Too bad you still have to pay for a portion of it out of your check. For many Americans, benefits are almost a fifth of their take-home pay.

**4. Micro-managing boss.** So, you have been doing your job for ten years, and your boss just graduated college. Sure, she knows more than you. That's why they hired her to tell you what to do. Well, if she wants to micro-manage and be involved in every detail, why doesn't she just do it herself. There are a lot better things that you could be doing with your time.

**5. Pay not commensurate with your work.** So, you worked sixty hours this week. Thanks. We really appreciate that. Even more, we appreciate the fact that you are a salaried employee, so we do not have to pay overtime. When we do the math, you averaged about sixty work hours per week each week this month, so even with your great salary, you actually earn about $12.00 per hour.

**6. Management not sensitive enough to employee concerns.** Perhaps you had someone close to you pass away, and you wanted to attend the funeral. Hopefully, you have enough leave or vacation accumulated to take the time off. Even then, there is a limit to the amount of time that you will be allowed to grieve. Maybe your child is going through a particularly traumatic time in his life and you would like to be able to visit the school more or volunteer more. Check your accumulated time-off balance!

**7. Managers displays favoritism towards other employees.** Is it your fault that you never learned how to make small talk around the water cooler? Does that mean that you shouldn't be given the same opportunities as the brown-nosers? Or maybe you were not born with a face and figure like Beyoncé. Does that mean that your stunning co-worker should be treated better than you?

**8. Lack of flexibility in daily scheduling.** For those people with children, this is a big deal. Not having the ability to attend conferences, school activities, and special occasions is a really big deal.

**9. No ownership in a company that you helped build.** In many instances, anything you invent or create is not yours. It's the property of the company you work for when you're creating it.

**10. No authority to solve problems as you see fit.** For most employees, if the solution doesn't fit inside of the corporate box, there is nothing you can do to help clients and customers, even when you want to.

## *Making a difference*

When most people think of entrepreneurship a few things come to mind, owning your own business, making your own money, controlling your time and your efforts. Most people won't necessarily relate entrepreneurship to the concept of living out your purpose. It has been my experience that when most people talk about living out your purpose, helping others, and making the world a better place, they tend to think about non-profit social justice type of pursuits. Seldom do people associate becoming an entrepreneur to making the world a better place. In fact, the thing that most people relate entrepreneurship to is making money.

I believe that entrepreneurship is more about living out your purpose and following your destiny, than it is about making money. It seems that making money comes second to purpose. Stop for a moment and think of all the things that business and business ideas that have been invented and brought to market in your lifetime. Companies like Microsoft, Apple, Uber, and even Coca-Cola were once the fledgling ideas of start-up entrepreneurs. And I think it is safe to say that these companies have made the world a better place.

Let's take the example of Uber a step further. A friend of mine is an attorney and he practices DUI Defense. Every day he defends people who have been charged with Driving Under the Influence of drugs and or alcohol. Driving while under the influence has destroyed many lives. Some of those lives are the victims of the DUI perpetrators that were involved in accidents. And some of those lives are of the family and friends of DUI perpetrators who lose time with family members when they are convicted of DUI.

Enter UBER, the ride sharing company that has all but obliterated the taxi cab industry. Because of UBER's model of inexpensive rides combined with technology has greatly helped reduce the number of DUI's. It is now easier and cheaper than ever to request an UBER after a night of drinking. My colleague that I mentioned earlier verified this. He told me once that UBER is ruining his business. He has far fewer clients than ever before. While this is great for families, it's not so good for DUI attorneys. But the point that I am making is that many times a small idea can become a big idea that has the capacity to change the world we live in. And while it may be a bad thing for my DUI friend, overall, it's a great thing for society. Perhaps, I will send him a copy of this book and encourage him to start a new business considering that his current one seems to be headed downhill.

In the UBER example, the founders found a higher purpose in their business, saving lives. Purpose comes first, then the business. Sometimes this sense of purpose can cause entrepreneurs to think of some pretty strange ideas. No matter how crazy your business idea seems, what you do is up to you.

This reminds me of one of the craziest businesses ventures that I can recall. In 1965, a student at Yale wrote a paper about the transportation industry and how it would be better with a more centralized form of distribution. He described shipping all packages to a central hub and then dispersing them across the country. Initially the professor, his colleagues and, investors thought the guy was crazy and gave little credence to his idea. Legend has it that he even received a failing grade for the paper he wrote in college.

To make a long story short, the company was FedEx, and the student was Fred Smith, founder. I don't need to tell you how that business worked out. That story alone should give you a few billion reasons to keep going on this journey. The only limitation in entrepreneurship is the one you place on yourself.

Some people start businesses for financial gain. Others start businesses after traumatic events. And still others start businesses because of layoffs and necessity. Of all the reasons that people start business, the necessity for some level of personal fulfilment and financial stability is usually toward the top of the list. As we have already discussed, many of the common workplace complaints in chapter 2 motivate people to become entrepreneurs. I have found that there are five primary reasons that people start businesses. They are to pursue their purpose, have career freedom, express their individuality, financial freedom, and to create a legacy for their family. Ideally, entrepreneurs want more of all five equally. Let's talk about how entrepreneurship benefits the entrepreneur and helps her fulfill her purpose.

## *Personal fulfilment*

Entrepreneurship can lead to huge financial successes, but the likelihood of an entrepreneur getting rich from an upstart is very slim.

As a rule of thumb, don't let financial success be your motivating factor for any venture.

The first business that I started was a partnership with two other entrepreneurs. We started a small manufacturing company that produced a patented product for the cosmetology industry. I was very excited about the new venture and having my name on a patent. In all honesty, I was more excited about being in business than the business or should I say industry that I was in. But I had no real passion for the product that we created. Our primary goal was to sell a lot of them and make some serious money.

To make a long and painful story short, after some initial success we ended up shutting down after a couple of years. I think one reason that we, or more importantly I was not as successful with this venture was because I had no real level of personal fulfillment with what we were doing. Not that anything was wrong with what we were doing, I just wasn't that interested in the cosmetology industry. One of my partners was very interested in the industry and this showed in his passion for the product and the business. Even after we shut down, he continued to try and make things work.

Your first and foremost source of motivation should be personal fulfillment. Your venture should satisfy some purpose for your life. When we talk about purpose and personal fulfilment, we do not have to necessarily think about very high and lofty things like "saving the world." Your purpose can be based on the things that you think are important and things that give you a sense of accomplishment.

I have a friend who is a baker and can bake some of the best cakes that I have ever tasted. But if you were to look at him you would think that he was more a mechanic than a baker. He is a big guy with a thick beard and a deep voice. In fact, the first time that I met him was in a dimly lit hallway. To be honest I didn't know if he was going to beat me up or rob me. When he approached, I was waiting for what he would say or do. He asked me if I wanted a piece of cake. Shocked, but intrigued, I said yes. He proceeded to give me a piece of the tastiest cake that I had ever had.

This baker also had a purpose. He truly felt that he could help spread love by baking and selling cakes to others. For him, each piece of cake brought smiles and happiness to those that ate it. His cakes brought joy to thousands of people and hundreds of parties across the city. At first glance you would think that he was just a baker. But if you dug a little deeper you saw that he was committed to his craft and the excellence of his product. And it was clear with the results that he received from his cakes. He did not start with the thought of how much money he could make. In fact, he usually threw away more cakes than he kept, because they did not meet his standards.

His purpose was to spread and share love. He just chose baking as the vehicle to do that. In fact, his slogan was "Taste Love."

## *Career freedom*

Career freedom ranks high on the list of reasons to pursue entrepreneurship. Whether your purpose is directly related to your business or not, one thing is for sure, if you do not have the freedom to pursue your purpose, you will never achieve it. There are not many jobs that allow people the freedom to work and pursue their purpose or dreams. In fact, many jobs seem more apt to deter you from your purpose and destroy your dreams.

For entrepreneurs, jobs that do not align with their ideals are drudgery. In fact, for me personally, in the past working jobs that have no alignment with my purpose are a slow death. Entrepreneurship allows you an opportunity to really be free career wise. When you are your own boss you can try different ideas, create new concepts, and experiment with what makes you happy. Of course, ample consideration should be given to the desires of your clients and what they like and want. But overall you are free to express yourself and your abilities.

## *Expressing your uniqueness*

Some people decide to try entrepreneurship so that they can express their own personal uniqueness. Many entrepreneurs have a passion, product, or service that is intimately connected to them as individuals. For them, entrepreneurship becomes a natural extension of who they are. Think about artists, artisans, and inventors who primarily have started businesses to market and sell their works. These creatives are also entrepreneurs, although we often do not think of them in that way.

Nonetheless they make the world a better place through expressing their uniqueness as individuals.

Earlier we mentioned Uber and the effect it has had on the market. If you have ever used or worked for Uber, one of the greatest things about Uber is the people. I use Uber on a regular basis and must say that I always meet some of the most interesting drivers. Once I even drove Uber for a week just to see how the experience was from the other side. To my astonishment, it was just as good. I met some amazing riders with very interesting personalities.

This unique business came from a unique group of entrepreneurs and has created a unique experience. Think for a moment of all the other unique businesses like Uber that have sprung up and how they have changed the landscape. The numerous app companies, website companies and online graphics companies have made it even more possible for individual entrepreneurs to express their uniqueness through using the unique products of others.

## Financial Freedom

Financial freedom ranks high on the list of reasons that people pursue entrepreneurship. There are two ways to look at the financial freedom perspective. One is that running your own business allows you to be in control of how much, or how little you make. Your salary is dependent upon what you think is important. When you work for others, you have very little say in what or how you get paid.

Another form of financial freedom, derived from entrepreneurship, is the freedom created by having enough money to do the things that you think are important. For instance, if it is important to you that you support charitable causes, entrepreneurship can help with that. Again, looking at this concept of personal fulfillment, if one of your goals is to help others, you need money. Kind words, thoughts, and even volunteering all help a great deal, but most charitable causes need money more than anything.

In fact, this aspect of financial freedom has somewhat of a related effect on charitable causes. The more money that the charity has, the more freedom that they themselves have. Money used wisely can do so much good. If used correctly, it has a perpetual effect to help so many other people become free.

## Legacy living

The last benefit of entrepreneurship that I'll cover has a more long-term horizon for fulfillment. It's legacy living. It assumes that an entrepreneur has decided to start a business so he or she can build a tangible business legacy to pass on for generations. Inherent in that legacy is the concept of wealth creation, but just as important in this concept of legacy, are the concepts of character development and integrity for the foundational strength of the family.

There are numerous examples of entrepreneurs who, by happenstance or deliberately, created legacies that remain today.

Many of us know these names and the stories of these businesses (Rockefeller, Ford, American Telephone and Telegraph (ATT), Coca-Cola, McDonald's, etc.). However, we often fail to remember that, at some point in their entrepreneurial journeys, they were small businesses just like yours.

Years from now, other businesses we can easily recall will have a legacy impact: Apple, Microsoft, Berkshire Hathaway. These businesses were started in the last fifty years. And all were started from the most meager beginnings. They are now some of the most lucrative businesses and wealthiest entrepreneurs in the world. Not only have they created a financial legacy, they have also created a legacy of inventions, technologies, products, and services. What type of world would we live in if the founders of these great companies had chosen not to heed the entrepreneurial call?

While your entrepreneurial legacy may not be as grand as some of the ones that I have mentioned above, it is no less important to your family. Entrepreneurship can provide a lasting sense of pride for your family as well as money. There is also the legacy of the body of entrepreneurial knowledge that you can pass on to your family. And this knowledge is sometimes more valuable than money.

# Chapter 4

## Strong Mind, Body and Spirit = Strong Business

*"You are your most important asset and you can't afford to take a loss. You must take care of your mind, body and spirit. If you don't then who will?"*

*– Kevin R. McGee*

## Three Things to Think About

1. Entrepreneurs are regular people and all people have three primary components, mind, body and spirit. All three must be in good condition to have total success.

2. Taking time to grow yourself is just as important as taking time to grow your business.

3. It does little good if your business is financially successful and you are in bad health. Good money and bad health is always bad.

## *Strength and internal fortitude*

Entrepreneurship and small business ownership are demanding pursuits by any standards. Ask almost any entrepreneur how much they work and the answer will generally be the same. In the early years of your business, you should be prepared to live and breathe your business. In the early years, it is going to take some time to build your business.

There will be many mental, physical, and spiritual demands on you. The latter is the source of some debate. There are some who question, the importance of spirituality and the belief in higher powers, to successful entrepreneurship. But there are numerous studies that show that the majority of successful entrepreneurs admit to believing in a higher power and certain aspects of spirituality. And let's be clear there is a difference between spirituality and organized religion. Spirituality in this context has no set preference of religious sect. It doesn't matter that you believe in something specific. What matters is that you believe in something.

Wherever you draw your strength and inspiration from, it should be a source that has the power to sustain you for the duration of your start-up stage and beyond. You must have the strength to develop all your latent characteristics such as fortitude, humility, persistence, perseverance. And my personal favorite, patience.

While entrepreneurship can be a part of fulfilling your purpose, what happens when things don't go as planned? Yes, the sky is the limit for entrepreneurship and almost anything is possible, but it's a long fall when or if things go wrong. Nothing in life is assured, and success can't be assumed -- particularly in the field of entrepreneurship. With entrepreneurship, you must be prepared to accept failure along with success. Any savvy entrepreneur who has become successful will tell you that for every successful venture, there have been numerous failures. In fact, it is often from these failures that entrepreneurs develop the ideas, products, or inventions that eventually lead them to the overall success.

Have you ever been sitting at the dinner table with your wife and toddler and heard someone bang on your door around 6:55 p.m. on a dark winter evening? Neither had I until it happened to me. When I cautiously went to the door to see who it was, I was relieved to find out that it was a member of the local law enforcement community. A county marshal's deputy to be exact. I did not know it before that day, but in addition to safeguarding our communities, the county marshals were also responsible for serving defendants with subpoenas for law suits. I was getting sued.

This learning experience came after my first business closure. I had decided to open a restaurant by myself, without having ever fully operating one for myself or with the help of anyone else. Sure, I had worked in restaurants throughout my youth and in college. But I'd never owned one, and I didn't intimately know anyone who had owned one. But I was pretty smart, or so I thought. Smart enough to be successful in the most difficult industry with the highest failure rate? It was a prime example of entrepreneurship gone bad. (Remember when I talked about evaluating the real potential for success?)

At any rate, a couple of tough years followed as my family tried to rebound from this "learning experience." If you want to know how to lose $100K in a year, just open a restaurant. See, there can be immense financial risks associated with entrepreneurship. So, undertaking this type of endeavor is not for the faint of heart and should not be done unadvisedly. With any venture, there will always be some level of risk. Whether that's financial, reputational, physical, or mental. But, as an entrepreneur, you must try to mitigate that risk as much as possible. You must develop the internal fortitude to handle the types of situations that are inevitable.

## *The confidence to create change*

There is a certain level of confidence and bravado present in almost every entrepreneur and small business owner that I have ever met. A willingness to go against the odds. A willingness to accept the challenge to do the impossible. Certainly, more unsuccessful entrepreneurs than we could count have been born and passed away without the world ever knowing of their contribution. That does not diminish their contribution to our society.

Can you imagine where we would be today without these entrepreneurs? Well, we would be walking everywhere, because we would have no cars. There would be no lights or electricity. No Happy Meals or iPads, or iPhones. (Oh, my God! No iPhones.)

What if no one desired a better, easier way of life? Our ancestors from 6,000 years ago, in the Mesopotamian region, were sitting around wondering how much better life would be if they did not have to drag around bushels of grain. This imaginative need for an easier way to transport products and people gave way to the concept of the wheel in around 3,000 BC.

One day an ancient inhabitant was sitting around and happened to see a smooth round rock roll effortlessly down a hill. Our maybe a child was playing with smooth, round pebbles and noticed how effortlessly they moved around compared to other jagged rocks. Can you imagine what the other members of that child's ancient community were saying when she began to craft the prototype for the wheel? I'd bet they thought he or she was crazy! Why would you want to roll things around, when you could just carry it?

Yet, this inventor of old pushed on and created the technology that would allow countless generations of inventors and entrepreneurs to capitalize on the wheel – a technology that is present in virtually everything we use today. What could be created today without the wheel? The wheel and its circular motion is more than something used for transport. It is the conceptual basis for gears, pulleys, levers, locomotion, and most importantly, timekeeping.

So, having the confidence to not only think about your ideas but put them into motion is crucial. You must have confidence that your idea will make a substantive change in your life and others. The need and demand for change has existed since the beginning and will always exist as long as we continue to exist. Entrepreneurs are always the ones on verge of that change.

## *Facing the financial consequences*
As an entrepreneur, you'll find that there are some very specific financial consequences for starting your own business. It is not inconceivable that you could literally lose everything you own in the pursuit of your entrepreneurial dream. In fact, many people have done just that. So, when you're considering entrepreneurship, you must be willing to face the potential financial consequences related to such a risky venture. There is no amount of planning or preparation that can fully insulate you from the possibility of financial failure.

However, you can attempt to mitigate the impact of this financial consequence for you and your family. One of the key things that I tell entrepreneurs is that it's much easier for your business to be successful if you do not have to use the profit from your business to sustain your personal financial obligations. You should develop a strategy that allows you to reinvest money earned from your business into the business. In the beginning stages, your business is much like a newborn baby who needs constant feeding and attention. To think that your business will be self-sustaining from day one is just as ludicrous as believing that a newborn baby can be self-sustaining from the day it's born.

To best prepare yourself, you must do a few key things. The first is to have a very good idea of the cost of not only starting your business but also maintaining it for at least six months. In doing this projection, you should allow extra room for unexpected expenses. The next thing that you can do to position yourself is to, if possible, identify an alternate source of revenue to help provide for your personal financial obligations. This can come in the form of spousal support, keeping your day job, or using personal savings. In general, I do not advocate borrowing money to start your business. If you must borrow money to start any aspect of your business, you are already beginning your venture with debt and decreasing the ability of your business to be successful.

## *Facing personal failure*

Another thing to consider is the possibility of personal failure. Failure is not a bad word. It simply means that you tried something and it didn't work out. It doesn't mean that you're a bad person or that you lack intelligence. It just means that perhaps you've made some mistakes or poor decisions. Or it could mean that something shifted in the market that was beyond your control to cause the failure. The bottom line is that you can't take failure personally.

There are entrepreneurs who have had failed ventures and have internalized this failure. One thing that I have come to realize over the years is that you, we are never failures. So, there is no need to internalize any failures in entrepreneurship or in any part of our lives. The things we try fail. The business we start fail. The relationships that we have fail. But if we continue to try and we continue to move forward we are never failures.

Maybe you've been unsuccessful at entrepreneurship in the past, so you have yet to launch out again. You still have that yearning in your spirit to give it one more shot, though. I would encourage you to move past your personal failure and begin to identify how you can learn from your mistakes and move forward with your vision.

Novice entrepreneurs are often overly optimistic when things are going well and overly self-critical when things are going wrong. You should try and keep an even perspective in successes and failures. They are two sides of the same coin and each depends upon the other to add perspective to the venture and provide knowledge and wisdom to you the entrepreneur. The only people that never fail are those that never try. Which would you rather be, one who tries and fails or one who fails to try?

## *Health, wellness, meditation and money*
When I say meditation here, it is intended to suggest finding a higher consciousness – and this does not have to be relegated to a particular culture or religion. Wikipedia defines meditation as "a broad variety of practices that includes techniques designed to promote relaxation, build internal energy or life force and develop compassion, love, patience, generosity, and forgiveness." So, what does meditation have to do with making money?

It's often odd to see the words "money" and "meditation" together. In fact, many of us believe that money and the act of meditating have nothing to do with each other.

With regards to entrepreneurship, it has been my experience that it is crucial for true success. I have found that the acts of meditation, praying, and reciting mantras have greatly helped my ability to overcome many obstacles in business ownership

It helps to keep a person balanced and centered. I have found that when I am balanced, more opportunities and ideas come to me. Entrepreneurship is a very stressful pursuit and requires a great deal of mental and physical stamina. Taking time to mentally and spiritually recharge makes a huge difference.

Equally important is exercising and nutrition. Many people think little of these things when planning to start their venture. Let me tell you that good health and good nutrition is a must. Your body is the vehicle that you use to accomplish everything on this earth, everything! If it is in any state of disrepair, it won't work.

Think of it like this how far could you drive if your car had no gas and needed mechanical work done. You would not feel safe travelling more than a few miles. You would be concerned that you would run out of gas or break down on the side of the road. Well the true is same of your body and its ability to function at an optimal level.

Starting a business means that you should operate at an optimal level on a regular basis. There is no one there to pick up the slack so you must be in great physical shape to do this. I remember when I owned several restaurants in the late 90's. I was working 15 plus hours a day and eating very sporadically. And when I did it, it was often sugar laden foods that kept me charged up, but left me depleted nutritionally. I distinctly recall being in bad physical shape. I had stomach issues and was always tired and lethargic. Sometimes I would come home and my family would look at me and try to figure out if I was going to just pass out.

Trust me that is no way to live and no way to run a business. If I knew then what I knew now, I would have spent more time engaging in mediation, exercise, prayers, mantras and eating right. Today I incorporate these things in my business model. Good health and nutrition is a part of my business plan. I realize that my body and I are my company's most important asset, and I must take care of it. So, in addition to making sure I reach my business goals, I make sure I reach my health and wellness goals.

When you look at some of the most successful entrepreneurs in the country today, you will often learn that each of them incorporate health and wellness into their business models. Tony Robbins, the famed motivational speaker and entrepreneur, has been very open about the practice of meditation and its effect on business and entrepreneurship. Steve Jobs, the late co-founder of Apple, also was an advocate of meditation. As is Phil Night, founder of Nike. Russell Simmons, CEO and founder of Def Jam Records is an avid yoga practitioner. Oprah Winfrey also advocates health, wellness and meditation. She is reported to have offered meditation training to employees who desire it. Finally, Arianna Huffington, president and editor-in-chief of Huffington Post Media Group, is a big advocate for meditation and its ability to help positively impact the business world.

These are all billionaire business people and most of them were start-ups and first generation entrepreneurs just like you. There's some conventional wisdom about how to be as successful as these entrepreneurial moguls. Simply model certain aspects of their behavior. Research it for yourself and you will see that each of them and many others maintain a balanced life-style. This balance is often what gives them the business edge that they need to be successful. If you have ever seen any of them speak, they are always well balanced, well measured and very deliberate in their thoughts and actions. Such certainty comes from being completely in tune with one's self.

## *Patience, persistence, and perseverance*

My three favorite attributes of strength are patience, persistence and perseverance. Without question these are three of the hardest attributes to acquire and maintain. You may not immediately think of them as forms of strength. But if you think about it, how much strength and discipline does it take to exercise patience, persistence and perseverance? I will answer that for you, a lot.

If being a successful entrepreneur were easy, everyone would do it. Many would be successful entrepreneurs don't make simply because they are not persistent with the business. They do not persevere and many do not have the patience to keep going when things seem to not be progressing.

Over the last 20 years I have been sued by creditors after failed business ventures, at risk of losing my home pledged as collateral for a large business loan, contemplated bankruptcy, and strained my family relationships when working too much. I could go on but I think you get the idea. At any one of these challenging junctures I could have easily said I give it, I quit. And if I am honest with myself I did think about quitting. But, I didn't. I kept going. If I hadn't pushed through, I would likely not be writing this book today. I would likely not be fulfilling my purpose.

The following story is a true one, as are all the others, though I have changed the names to protect people's privacy. I have a business colleague named John that owns a financial services firm that bids on employee retirement plans for large cities. In the early years of his firm, he had an equal partner in the firm named Frank. After several years of trying to win a large city bid, his partner Frank decided that he had had enough and literally quit the partnership and renounced any further ownership. He could not pursue his dream anymore and he had lost his patience with the venture. He wanted nothing more to do with the business.

Reluctantly, my friend John, somehow found the money to buy Frank out. John was all in and committed to making the business work, no matter what. Then something amazing happened. Literally, the next week after John bought out Frank's ownership interests, my colleague John received news that the company had won a major city contract worth over $1million dollars.  That's right $1million dollars. This contract was the catalyst to create a very successful financial services firm that today is worth millions of dollars. Wow, what a difference a few days make.

But none of this would have happened if John gave up. He could have easily decided to quite once his partner did. But John was committed to being successful. And even after this major contract, John's business still had its share of ups and downs. Sometimes he almost lost everything, but he has stuck with it and reaped the benefits of his success.

Whether this is your first venture or your fourth, you should keep going. Entrepreneurship is more of a lifestyle choice and a lifelong journey than a one-time start-up event. Entrepreneurship is as largely about patience, persistence and perseverance. It is something that you must commit to from the beginning. If your tolerance for business losses is one failure, and you aren't willing to commit for the long term, then don't waste your time or your money!

## ☼ Success Secrets

Human beings are multi-dimensional. Everything about our physical make-up is intended to interact with and be a part of the environment we live in. We have eyes to see color variations, ears to hear sounds, noses to smell aromas, and sensory nerves in our skin to feel touch. That's why it is so odd that we try to separate our physical bodies from the intangible things that we interact with, like light, smells, and sounds.

As an entrepreneur, I would encourage you to become well rounded. You should eat right, exercise, meditate, pray and think positive thoughts about yourself and others. Through doing these things your entire being becomes strong. And it is this strength that allows you to better develop your patience, persistence, and perseverance. This will give you an edge in business that some others may not have.

# Chapter 5

## Balancing family, friends and entrepreneurship

*"With regards to family, they say that blood is thicker than water. Well that may be true, but spilled blood is a lot harder to clean up."*

*– Kevin R. McGee*

### Three Things to Think About

1. The rewards of owning your own business are great. But it is not worth the risk of damaging the relationships with loved ones. You will have to be deliberate and work on keeping your relationships with those you love intact.

2. Entrepreneurship is demanding, and you must give a lot of consideration to the demands and determine the right time to start your business.

3. If done correctly creating a family legacy of entrepreneurship can create positive change that lasts a life-time. Conversely, if handled recklessly family entrepreneurship can create just as much of a negative change.

## *Establishing family and work balance*

Of all the things that require special attention when starting your business, understanding the effects of entrepreneurship on relationships is crucial. We are human beings and relationships are a huge part of what makes us tick. Although the word *entrepreneur* infers a singular person, entrepreneurship is definitely not an individual pursuit. Whether you are married, in a relationship, or have close friends and family, all your relationships will be affected by your decision to start a business. Regardless of how strong you think your relationships are, they will be tested.

I have already mentioned a few of my tests, particularly with my wife and children. But I could give you dozens of more stories involving family and friends, and how my entrepreneurial pursuits have affected my relationships positively and not-so-positively. But through this life-long process I have picked up a few tips that can help you better manage your relationships and keep the people you love and care for close to you, as much as possible.

The one thing that I will say upfront and that I want you to remember is that you must become very comfortable early on realizing that not everyone will be happy with your entrepreneurial pursuits all the time. And not everyone will be supportive. But it's not necessarily that they want to see you do bad, some people are just more fearful than supportive. And they try and cast their well-intentioned caution and concern on you. But you must make sure that you don't let this stifle your enthusiasm for starting your business.

Being an entrepreneur and operating a small business can create havoc within a family. Some of us may know someone who started a business, which subsequently failed, and whose family has paid the price. We could cite just as many examples where people have started businesses and become successful only to find that success can also cause a significant amount of stress on a family. More time working in the business and making money, sometimes means less time at home making the spouse and children happy.

Therefore, it is important that you establish a work/life balance. That means that you should make a deliberate attempt to ensure that you spend enough time with your business, but not too much and that you spend enough time with your family, but not too much. This can require you to make some tough decisions. When considering whether you should attend a networking function or your daughter's violin recital, there are many things to consider. For instance, if you were to attend the networking function, it could possibly lead to a client whose business would help you pay for a new violin for your daughter. It's a tough call, and there is no easy answer.

One answer is to create an environment within your family that includes everyone in the decision-making process of how time will be spent in a general sense. You should set aside specific times for your family that you can all agree on as family time. And you should make every attempt to honor this family time. By engaging the family in the process, everyone can express their feelings. Also, agreeing on how responsibilities around the house will be shared is crucial to creating a harmonious environment.

Another strategy is to include your family in the business at times. There will be times, regardless of the type of business, that your family can assist. Even if it is just giving you an opinion about a possible business deal or prospect. You must make sure that you engage your family, if they want to be engaged. I have involved my family in all my businesses and we are a stronger family as a result. Whether they have folded brochures, passed out business cards, or packed products in boxes, they have had fun being engaged. And they have learned some great lessons without even knowing it.

You should take great care in explaining your business and the opportunities that it presents to your family so that they clearly understand that the sacrifices you make are for them and for a better life. They should know the reasons why you are doing what you are doing. Do you remember the 5 W's that we discussed earlier? This is a prime opportunity to use a few of them. You should be sure that you acknowledge that through their support of the entrepreneurial vision, all members of your immediate family are truly your partners.

### *Spouse and children, stress and strain*
If you are married, it is imperative that your spouse buys into the idea when you make the decision to become an entrepreneur. And if you are not married, but plan to be married to your current partner, it might be a good idea to let him or her know of your future ambitions if you have any inkling that you want to be an entrepreneur. Save yourself a lot of pain and anguish down the line. Have very frank and candid conversations with your partner.

We have all heard stories about the effects of entrepreneurship on marriages. There are fights about money, time-management, household duties, ceasing marital relations, and just plain old being mad at the entrepreneurial spouse for choosing this difficult route. And from the entrepreneur's perspective, there's discord at times about a spouse's perceived lack of understanding and support. Sometimes when the business fails the marriage fails along with the marriage. Sometimes there are children involved and this makes for a very bad situation.

Early in my entrepreneurial career I was in the hospitality industry, as I mentioned earlier. When I made the decision one day to open a restaurant, I was dating my future wife. But even when we were dating I had a heart-to-heart conversation with her about what this new endeavor would require. And she decided to support me 100%, which I am so grateful to her for doing. That meant a lot to me during this time. And true to form, she was in the kitchen washing dishes and cooking. All of this while in law school herself.

It is of the utmost importance that you consider this impact on your family and that you properly prepare for it. One of the easiest ways to prepare for this is to have candid discussion with all members of your immediate family, regardless of their age. It is vital that you have everyone in your family on board and supportive of your decision to be an entrepreneur. This is not to say that your spouse or other members of your immediate family must be "all in" so to speak. They, at the least, must agree with your decision to pursue entrepreneurship.

If pursuing entrepreneurship is something you feel you must do but, after all attempts, you cannot gain the support of your spouse or significant other, perhaps you should have a larger conversation about your relationship. It is almost impossible to be successful at running a small business if you don't have the support of your significant other, spouse and children, if you have them. And it is not feasible or advisable that you try to go it alone and prove to them, through your successes, that they should support your decision.

If you feel that you must become an entrepreneur and you don't have the support of your family, my suggestion would be that you wait and spend more time educating them and persuading them to be supportive of your decision. Some ways that you can do this is by engaging them in the planning of your venture well before you pull the trigger.

In entrepreneurship, there are no guarantees, and for many people this is a hard proposition. If you were working a corporate job, you would be guaranteed a check every two-weeks, which does a lot to provide some level of stability for the household. And if you do your job, work hard and come to work regularly, for the most part, you can be assured that your employment will continue.

But with entrepreneurship you can work hard and give everything that you have and still fail. You can visit 50 potential clients in week and still make no sales. This inconsistent revenue stream can create a perceived lack of security for a family or spouse. This financial uncertainty is perhaps the toughest to handle. But if you have an open conversation with your spouse before taking this step and you both get on one accord, this can greatly reduce the amount of discontent. Also, if you try and plan for your start-up by creating an emergency fund this can help greatly.

The amount of time that you may have to spend away from your family could be a lot, depending on the type of business that you start. It is not uncommon for entrepreneurs to spend sixty to eighty plus hours per week working in their businesses. Much more than you would likely spend if you were working a regular job. And it is not possible to make more hours in the day, so where will you find the time to spend with family and friends? The lack of time consideration is an important one. If you are thinking that in the beginning stages of your business that you will be able to have an open schedule, you may want to think about that again.

This time commitment can be the source of great contention in a relationship, particularly if you are married. Your spouse will have to pick up the slack for familial commitments if you are busy with the business. In the beginning stages of your new business, the excitement of it is generally enough to keep peace around the home. But what about after you have been at it for a couple of years and your business still requires an enormous amount of your time?

Once you start your business you need to be comfortable with the fact that your business will always be on your mind, and there will almost always be something that you must do with it daily – particularly when your business first starts. When you are the business owner, there are no off days. If there is a problem with your business, it's always your responsibility to find the solutions. If you take a vacation or take off from work, no one will cover for your, assume your responsibilities or do your work while you are away.

A business is like a new born baby. If you have children, you understand the type of time commitment that I am talking about. Just like a new baby, a new business needs constant care and attention. It needs to be fed by your revenues, which will help it grow. It needs to be tended to when a mess is created. And there will certainly be times when you must clean up some metaphorical poop.

There are so many variables and potential challenges when starting and running a business, that it is almost impossible to address everything. But keeping the lines of communication open with your spouse and children is crucial to being able to navigate them successful with minimal damage to your relationships.

## *It's a family affair*

One would think that close family and friends would be your biggest cheerleaders when you decide to become an entrepreneur. But this is not always the case. In some instances, our closest family and friends are the ones who tell us that we cannot succeed. People think about the possibilities in life based on their own pasts and experiences. And if there are no entrepreneurs in their pasts, it is difficult for them to conceptualize this endeavor. So, they are sometimes more pessimistic than optimistic. There are many reasons that this pessimism takes place.

One reason, and perhaps the easiest to digest, is that the ones who love us the most want to try to protect us from harm and disappointment. They have seen the consequences of taking risks.

They have seen or heard of relationships broken up, homes disrupted, and substantial sums of money lost by some pursuing entrepreneurship.

Then you have those who have never tried anything outside of the norm. They have always worked a nine-to-five job, as did their parents, and perhaps grandparents. So, this idea of entrepreneurship is foreign to them. They aren't supportive because they don't know how to be. They don't understand that instead of discouraging the dreams of an entrepreneur, they should help the entrepreneur take steps to ensure, as much as possible, that the venture will be a success.

Less palatable is another reason why people discourage entrepreneurs: jealousy and envy. Anecdotally we refer to these people as haters. Plain and simple, some people don't want to see you succeed because if you succeed it somehow makes them feel as if they are failing. They have a variety of reasons for feeling this way. One common one is that they are do not have the courage and conviction to pursue their own dreams. They have trapped themselves into a life that they do not enjoy, but they lack the gumption to change it. Jealousy is a hard thing to consider when thinking about our loved ones. But people fear and hate what they do not understand.

It is a sobering experience to think that your best friend, mother, father, sister, brother or others could be envious of you to the extent that he or she would like to see you fail. To see you live a mediocre life rather than pursue your passions. The unfortunate truth, though, is that if you are to succeed, you must remove negative forces from your life or, in some cases, use them as a source of motivation. However, it has been my experience that if you try to turn your haters into your motivators, it can sometimes have a detrimental effect on you, particularly if they are people that are close to you. You may begin to feel anger toward the ones you feel are not supporting you.

I have found that energy spent trying to deal with the constant barrage of negative comments takes more of a toll than just not including those people in your conversations and thoughts. Yeah, it seems like a lonely proposition to be unable to share your dreams and passions with the ones that you love, but sometimes that's the way it is. A better idea is to surround yourself with other entrepreneurs. There are any number of meet-up style groups, online resources, and blogs that cater to entrepreneurs. There you will find others who will support you because they know the issues that you face. Hopefully, as those close to you see that you cannot be deterred, they will change their attitudes and want to be a part of your success.

Conversely you may have family members who are supportive of you and your entrepreneurial dreams. Your family can be a great source of support and assistance in the early stages of your business. If willing, they can offer free or lower-cost labor. They can be trusted people to watch the shop while you are away. But, as with all situations, the expectations and compensation should be clear. You may believe that your mother is going to work for free, but the saying goes that there is nothing free in this world. It may not necessarily cost you money, but there is a cost involved in every transaction. She may have an expectation of a nicer-than-normal Mother's Day gift after working 100 unpaid hours over the past year. And to give her anything less than a great Mother's Day gift may mean the end to your labor pool. Be clear and reasonable about the expectations you have for your family members.

While having your family involved in your business can have great rewards, it can also be a source of great stress and frustration if clear boundaries and responsibilities are not set. First, you should remember that this is a small business. The key word is "business." And this endeavor is strictly about business. It is not about personal relationships or family relationships. Yes, relationships are good for business, but if I had a dollar for every business owner who has a non-performing family member working for him or her, I could retire today.

Simply put, there is no excuse for having a family member on the payroll – or any employee for that matter – who is not performing. The rules that you have for employees should be the same for your family; and if you are not strong enough to fire your mother, wife, brother, and sister, then they should not be working for you. Remember: Unless it is a true partnership situation, these family members are your employees anytime that they are in the business. Your other employees will look at how you treat your family members, and if there is any discrepancy in how you treat them versus your employees, you will have problems.

## *Generational benefits of entrepreneurship*
One of the things many entrepreneurs forget is that it generally takes at least two generations for a business to become extremely successful. While we often hear about companies making the leap from hundreds of thousands of dollars in sales to several million dollars in record time, this is more the exception than the norm. If you look at some of the most successful businesses in America, you will find that it has taken several generations and several iterations of the business to evolve to the stage that it is today. IF you look at the age of many of the household business names, you will find decades if not centuries of growth and development. Here are a few of them and the year that they were started; Cigna Insurance-1792, New York Stock Exchange-1792, Jim Beam Whiskey-1795, Colgate-1806, Brooks Brothers-1818, JP Morgan Chase-1799, Coca Cola-1892, Proctor and Gamble-1837. I could go on but I think you get the idea. Success takes time, building a business takes time, so you should be prepared to take time.

Success, in business and in life, is based on long-term strategy. Like investing, the longer you continually put in, the greater the return will be. To be clear, this does not necessarily mean that you continue with the same business model and type for generations. It means that your pursuit for entrepreneurial success should be a lifelong journey – and a family affair. Unbeknownst to most entrepreneurs, the biggest component of entrepreneurial success, besides an abundance of capital, is industry experience and entrepreneurial experience.

There are countless entrepreneurs who can trace their success back to conversations they overheard around the dinner table when they were children. I have a friend that is a second-generation commercial contractor. In many of the conversations that I have had with him, he vividly recalls the lessons he learned at the dinner table. Once he became of age and assumed his role in the family business, operating it was, surprisingly, an easy task. It was almost second nature. From listening to his family members and going to business meetings with his father, he had gained a wealth of knowledge.

He had observed his family's conversations about the business in good times and bad times. He experienced the pains and stresses of the lean times of the business. For him, this meant fewer school clothes, or perhaps less steak and more chicken on the dinner table. He even observed some of the conflict and let's call them "intense moments of fellowship" between his parents during these lean times. So, once he became an adult, got married, and assumed leadership of the company, he was prepared for whatever may come and knew that bad economic times did not mean the end of the business.

He knew most of his family business suppliers, vendors, and customers. He knew their habits, traits, likes, and dislikes. He knew the pricing and value of many of the supplies. He understood the basic business principles of supply and demand as well as customer service. After going to college, all he had to do was to add his knowledge to the pot, so to speak. With his new knowledge, he took the core values of his family business and added new technologies and processes that literally took the business to the next level. The important thing to note here is that Todd had a very short learning curve. He came into the business knowing all the basics of not only business, but also of a specific business niche.

While you are planning your business venture, keep the future in mind, and build a business that will stand the test of time. Trying to rush the development of a business for the sake of immediate personal gain is often a losing situation. Take a holistic approach to building your business. Work to make a profit but, more importantly, focus on creating stable systems and processes. Try and involve your family in your business if possible, even at an early age. My children began assisting me with my businesses around the age of four or five – and I don't mean just hanging out with me. I would have them working in one of my restaurants doing simple, educational tasks. One day they might be counting forks for tables, placing plates in equal-numbered stacks, or perhaps rinsing vegetables. As they became older, their responsibilities increased, and they would set tables, fold linen napkins, and place glasses.

I did not withhold anything from them. And while they were helping me, they would invariably assault me with a barrage of questions. Those of you with children know exactly what I mean. As I answered these questions, their little minds were being filled with indispensable knowledge. They'd ask, "Daddy, why did you give that man a business card?" or "Daddy, what is a business card?" or "Daddy, what is an invoice?" or "Daddy, what does customer service mean?"

By the time they were in elementary school, they were bona fide sales agents, and every teacher in the school had one of my business cards. I probably made an extra $5,000 from people at that school who used our catering company. It was really a win-win situation. And by involving them, it made them feel a part of the process while helping them understand why Daddy was gone a lot of the time. If they went with me on occasion, then they knew where I was and what I was doing.

As they got older and interacted with other children their age, people began commenting on how different they are. *Your children are so well organized and helpful. Your children always seem to take the lead in organizing the other children and making sure that everything goes well.* These sentiments that I've heard over the years are a function of them watching their parents and how we have operated our businesses. Even if they choose not to follow in our footsteps, they will have the knowledge base and legacy of a family business.

But, I was careful not to force them to learn anything. It was never an unpleasant experience. I seldom make them do things related to my businesses that they do not like to do. Instead I try to cater to their specific interests. My oldest daughter, for instance, loves graphics programs. So, I routinely would have her create PowerPoint® presentations for my business. While she was not sophisticated enough to do a professional-level presentation, she could put in the basic information and set up the slide transitions – starting when she was just ten years old. Now she is a pro. Children are truly amazing if you let them be.

## *Family and friends as employees*
Many start-ups depend heavily on family and close friends to help them with their businesses in the early stages. If this is an option for you, it could be a great way to reduce start-up labor costs. Family and friends may work for little or no money just to help you out. But be very cautious when making this decision. Because having your family and friends involved in the business can also have some very serious negative consequences, in addition to those we mentioned earlier.

The courts are filled with cases of family-owned businesses suing family members for stealing, cheating, and embezzling. A family business is first and foremost a business and nothing should be taken for granted. There should be rules, processes, and procedures for disbursements, payouts, free items, etc.

One way to mitigate potential problems with family members and money is to create solid processes and procedures for handling money and any other issues for that matter. Make it a habit to stay on top of what is going on in your business at all time. Do not make the mistake of assuming that because your family or friend is involved in your business, that all their actions will be beneficial to your business.

Even though the temptation of bringing your family on board to help in the beginning is a great financial help, I generally advise my clients to try to build the business using non-family labor. The stress of a new business by itself can tear a family or marriage apart. Add to that the possible stress and strain of working with a family member and you might have a recipe for disaster. If you are starting your business on a shoestring budget, the weight of the business is likely to break the shoestring. Financial issues are the leading cause of disagreements with family when it comes to business. Money is important but it is not worth losing your family.

## ✺ Success Secrets

Once you start your business, it will be easy for you to convince yourself that the long hours and sleepless nights are for the best. You will believe that your sacrifice will help you, your family, and your loved ones get further in the long run. While this may be true, your family must believe it as well.

If you try and go it alone and drag your family with you, and they are unwilling, you may look back and find them gone. You can't replace friends, family or relationships.

From day one you need to try to create some sense of balance between your life and your business. Yes, it may take a little longer to reach success, but you will reach it and still be whole. And isn't that the reason that you want to start a business? So that you live a happier, healthier, and fuller life?

Whether involving your family in your business creates a pleasant or unpleasant experience, the most important take away is remembering that family and the ones that you love are the most important things in life.

# Chapter 6

## The pros and cons of business partnerships

*"Two are better than one, because they have a good return for their labor: If either of them falls down, one can help the other up.*

*But pity anyone who falls and has no one to help them up."*

*-Ecclesiastes 4:9-10*

---

### Three Things to Think About

1. You should only enter business partnerships if have thoroughly discussed and considered all the potential issues.

2. Clearly and concisely document how your partnership will function. Written agreements of roles and responsibilities is a must.

3. For a partnership to be successful, each partner must bring something of value to the table. It could be money, expertise, relationships, etc. but each partner must provide value to the partnership.

## When does a partnership make sense?

Entrepreneurship can be a risky endeavor. One way to mitigate that risk is to consider partnering with someone. A partnership, when done correctly, can be a great thing. it allows you to share the risk and responsibility with another individual. When you split the risk, you also split the responsibility, the accountability, and the workload. One thing to remember, though, is that you also split the profits. This does not mean that you cannot be profitable, but it does mean that you need to be sure that your business will generate enough income to satisfy two masters.

You should also be clear whether this business is a source of needed income for both you and your partner or whether it is a source of passive, extra income. Not having this clear distinction could be disastrous. If one partner is using her share of the profits to pay her personal bills and keep the lights on at home, and the other partner is using his share of the profits to buy his big boy toys, the motivation for each is drastically different, and that could affect the approach to the business. My advice would be not to go into any business venture with a partner if either partner will depend on the proceeds of the business to pay for his personal expenses.

When you start a partnership and one or both partners are depending on profits from the business to pay for their personal expenses, this is almost a guaranteed disaster. The stress alone of starting a new business is enough, without the added financial stress of needing every dollar that you profit in the business. In the early stages of your business, pulling money out of the business is a losing proposition. Money is food for a new business. Do you remember our analogy of a baby being like a business used earlier in the book?

So, to take the baby example a step further, what happens when a couple has a new baby and they disagree on how the baby will eat, sleep, and be raised? If the couple or "partners" aren't in agreement or can't come to an agreement about every aspect of their child, what happens? So, if you are in a business partnership and you and your partner haven't discussed every aspect of the businesses operations, growth or direction what do you think will ultimately happen if there are disagreements?

Whether you are going into partnership with family or close friends, you should be sure to set some initial ground rules for how the partnership will work. Over the years, I have had several different types of partnerships. Some of them have been with close friends and they have been successful. Unfortunately, though, some of them have cost me close friendships and put strain on family relationships. If I could do it all again I would do things very differently. No business or venture is ever worth losing a valued friendship or family relationship.

## *Write it down and make it plain*

The first step of entering a partnership with anyone is to make sure that there is a clear expectation of what each partner will be responsible for doing. Since everyone is different and has a different personality, we tend to transmit and receive information differently. What one person is intending to communicate may not be received in the manner intended. So, the best thing to do when establishing partnerships is to write everything down and make it plain. Even before drafting a formal contract or operating agreement of who is responsible for what, the first step is to have a general understanding of how your partnership will work.

This could be as simple as a one-page document that outlines that one person is responsible for sales and another person is responsible for the marketing. This is, clearly, a very broad way to classify it, but it allows you to decide which activities fall into which buckets. Perhaps one person is responsible for the day-to-day operations and the other partner is responsible for all sales, marketing, and external activities.

Or, if you are further along in your business relationship, it may be necessary to have a more detailed outline of roles and responsibilities and how you are going to respond.

Additionally, when you document the various aspects of how you and your partner will work together, it is also important that you discuss how you plan to exit the business. At some point, one of the partners may decide to pursue other opportunities. In this case, it is crucial that you have a procedure for how the business will operate if a partner decides to leave either voluntarily or with encouragement. You should realize that your partnership will likely not last forever. As we grow and mature, our interests, needs, and desires change.

Once you write it down and make it plain, you should revisit this document and add to it as your business grows. You will find that as you do business with someone, you will learn even more about him or her. What you learn about one another may influence your need to better define roles and responsibilities. There is one thing that you both should be crystal clear on, though: The number one goal of your partnership is to grow a successful and sustainable business.

The legal implications of a partnership are an entirely different matter. When creating your corporate structure, many variables can impact how you are taxed and treated. Additionally, ownership percentages should be clearly defined.

## *Friends as partners*

You and your buddy have been friends for at least two decades. You two know almost everything about one another and can complete each other's sentences. Sounds like a perfect partnership. Or does it? When money, responsibility, and accountability are introduced into a friendship, it often does not turn out well. As friends, all that you were responsible for was being good, trusted companions. Your responsibilities included listening to your friend's vent and providing a shoulder to cry on. You were accountable for bringing an extra six pack for the game. As a partner, there are bills, deadlines, customer orders, and customer complaints, to consider. Now, your friendship is about so much more than enjoying each other's company. As great as the idea initially sounds, becoming business partners with a friend often ends up badly for all of those involved. It's not impossible, but it must be well thought out.

Before going full speed into your joint venture, try a test run, and perhaps start your business out slowly by doing a few demonstrations or presentations with an independent third party. After a few months of testing your business, you will find out how dependable and reliable you both are as it relates to the business. Better to find out early than after you have incurred the expenses of creating and filing your corporate structure, invested money, secured a location, purchased marketing materials, etc. If the scenario is not going to work, you will know very quickly.

Business journals are filled with stories of partnerships gone bad, and many of them started out with family and friends. After all, when you think about who you want to work with, total strangers never come to mind. Maybe they should. One advantage to partnering with strangers is that you have a completely objective analysis of their abilities. If proper due diligence is done before entering the partnership and you properly protect yourself from a legal perspective by establishing the correct corporate structure, you should be fine. As a matter of fact, the most successful partnership that I have had to-date has been with someone that I had known for only nine months when we partnered on a six million-dollar deal.

I have been on the other end as well, partnering with both friends and family with disastrous results. I had to fire my wife twice (but I always had to hire her back because she was the only one willing to work for me). Seriously, partnering with family members can be devastating. Heed my words, be cautious before going down this road.

## Spouses as partners

Partnerships between spouses merit a little more attention. Given the stakes and possible consequences to this all-important union, these types of partnerships should be entered with great caution. I think it can be assumed that if an individual starts a business and is married, by default his or her spouse is a partner of some sorts in the venture. In this instance, "partner" means someone who is helping support the vision of the entrepreneur by perhaps taking on additional responsibilities at home and in personal life. Let's talk more about a formal partnership with your spouse, though.

Entrepreneurs form official spousal partnerships for a variety of reasons. One of the most common is when individuals create partnerships with their spouse because the spouse is either a woman or a member of a specific demographic group. There are many incentives available for women, veteran-owned and minority-owned businesses. While it is advisable to take advantage of every opportunity available, you should seriously consider the motivations behind entering partnership with your spouse based solely on the potential for incentives. Although the programs generally give preference to women and minorities, it is only when they play a significant role in the management of the day-to-day operations of the company.

In general, spousal partnerships should operate just as any other partnership. Each partner should have a specific set of roles and responsibilities providing a clear understanding of the part they play in operating the business. The advantages to spousal partnerships are that your partner obviously understands the challenges and issues that you may have with your personal life. Additionally, if the spouses are part of the business in an official capacity, it is more likely that they will be more understanding when the demands of the business mean that you, as an entrepreneur, must spend more time in the business. It is also beneficial because it will perhaps allow a reluctant spouse to see the promise and potential in the business.

In spousal partnerships, each spouse should maintain a specific percentage of ownership in the company, just as with any partnership. This percentage should be documented in the organizational documents used when starting the business. It should also have some rational behind why which partner owns what percentage.

While there are benefits, there are also dire consequences if the business and/or partnership is not successful. The most significant consequence, as you may guess, is that sometimes spousal partnerships will end in divorce – from the business relationship as well as the marriage. Disagreements on the direction or operation of the business can lead to heated discussions that may blend into pre-existing family issues. While I do believe that creating a business is a central component of creating a family legacy, it should not be at the expense of the family.

The best way that I've seen to establish spousal partnerships is to very clearly define not only the business boundaries but also the family boundaries. If there is a prescribed hierarchy within the home, it does not necessarily have to be the same in the business. For example, if you have a traditional home model where perhaps the husband acts as the head of household, he may or may not be the head of the business. There are numerous examples of women-owned businesses where the husband plays only a small supporting role in the operation.

Additionally, it is always best that each partner focus on his or her strengths and not on where they believe they should be based on any sort of presumed hierarchy. If one spouse has an accounting background, it would make no sense for the other spouse to manage the fiscal affairs of the company. Make the determination of strengths and match them to roles. And once you have determined what the boundaries are for you and your spouse, make a committed effort to not cross those boundaries. Nothing is worth more than keeping your family together.

## Equally yoked

The concept of being "equally yoked" comes from a biblical and historical background. A yoke refers to a type of harness, hitch, or strap that is commonly used to connect to animals for the purposes of pulling an object. In business terms, it means that you and your partner are tied together and essentially share the same responsibility for the success and failure of a business. It also means that each person in the partnership should pull his or her weight. When two horses are yoked, or attached to, a carriage, both horses must pull with the same force at the same speed for the carriage to move forward. Both horses must constantly relate to one another and adjust their speed and pace so that they are in sync. If they don't do so, and one horse is pulling harder and faster than the other, then the carriage will either crash or travel in a circle. In partnerships where one partner is pulling most the weight, this exact phenomenon takes place.

When entering a partnership and you begin a business, you should expect that it will take some time for each partner to get acclimated to the other. Even if you have known your partner for a long time before starting the business, this does not mean that they will behave the same once the business starts. People behave differently and display different characteristics depending on the circumstances.

## Cross-cultural alliances

One of the things that I am a big advocate for is creating opportunities to engage people of other cultures at all levels in a variety of activities and enterprises. I think this engagement does a lot to enrich not only the people involved but it enriches the activity or enterprise itself. I believe that this is true for entrepreneurship as well. If we look back throughout history, we will see that this mindset is not new.

Since the beginning of recorded history, humanity has engaged in some form of trade and commerce among people of different cultures. Given the geographic locations of the various countries and their respective natural and produced resources, cross-cultural trade and interaction was necessary. Some countries were rich in mineral resources, while others had highly agrarian cultures. Others had textiles, furs, silks, etc. These different cultures routinely traded with one another for the betterment of their individual communities.

These types of trading activities often led to long-term amiable relationships and partnerships among people of different cultures. So, there is value in creating relationships and in this case partnerships with people of different cultures and ethnicities. While we no longer trade natural resources and produced goods, we can exchange culturally specific knowledge, expertise and perspective. America is a great country that has the benefit of having a large and diverse number of cultures that exist within her borders. It is a pity though, that more people do not look outside of their culture for potential partnerships.

Several years ago, I decided to look outside of my own culture to find business partners. I could find partners within my culture, but I felt it was important to broaden my own perspective and learn while contributing to others' learning experience. By chance, I befriended a Korean colleague close to my age through a contract on which I was working. Initially, our conversation centered on the nonprofit that he was working with, a Korean chamber of commerce.

As we developed our relationship, it gave me an opportunity to learn more about his culture and his perspective on the world. I provided the same insight for him, helping him to learn more about my culture. This has proved to be one of the best relationships that I have developed. It has given me a better perspective on how others do business and helped to break down some prejudices that I had based on my upbringing.

I have another business partner who is an older white-man. He and I have known one another for only a few years, at the time of writing this book. He too has proved to be a very good business partner and friend. We both have been able to have very candid conversations about our cultures and our perspectives on our partnership, entrepreneurship and life in general. This relationship has helped me to grow personally and professionally. But had I not deliberately sought it out, it is doubtful that the relationship with either of these individuals would have occurred.

I have several business partners who are of difference ethnicities. These relationships have been invaluable for several reasons. They have helped me become educated regarding some of the stereotypes that all people hold against other cultures. I have been able to have candid conversations with each of them about the differences in our cultures, and to my surprise, I learned that the bottom line is that the real differences are very few. Business is business.

Prejudices and racism continue to cause relational issues in this country. Racism is more than an attitude or perspective. It's a set of behaviors that I believe can be mitigated, in large part, via legislation. Racism is often easily identifiable. But prejudices are deep-seated in all of us, and they affect how we treat others every day. Often, we are not aware of our prejudices. And since many people do not consider themselves racists, they stop there. But while we may not be racist, we all have prejudices based on our upbringing and our environments. It's impossible not to have them.

Prejudices are largely influenced by how we were raised and influenced to view others. What does prejudice have to do with entrepreneurship? Plenty when you consider that as an entrepreneur you will have to deal with various types of people in the form of employees, clients, partners, and vendors. Moving past prejudices also allows you to grow and open your mind to the possibility of more business opportunities. If you are an African American and only look for African-American business partners or only target your business towards African Americans, you may be limited. If you are Korean and only target your business towards Koreans, again you are limiting yourself.

In my opinion there is no point in going into business if you only want to focus on one segment of the population for any aspect of your business needs. Now, if you target a particular group because of your niche, that is a different case. Then, you would be making a market data-driven conclusion about how you should reach your target audience. However, very few substantive niches are defined by culture or race.

I was so encouraged by my business dealings with my Asian counterpart that I began to look at other ethnicities as potential business partners. And today I am proud to say that I have business partners who are young, old, Korean, Canadian, African, Caucasian, gay, and lesbian. This has been intentional, to some degree, as should any business decision be. When you make decisions to reach out to other people as it relates to entrepreneurship, it should be with a specific goal in mind.

This does not mean that you should not also develop casual friendships. In my business dealings, the basic tenets of getting to know a person come first; but, you should have goals in mind when you associate with people. Whether those goals are to learn more about their ways of doing business or whether they are to learn if there are any cultural norms and mores that would affect the way you market to a particular audience. Be deliberate.

For most of us, the thought of having a business partner is a little frightening -- especially if you do not already have someone in mind. So, the thought of creating cross-cultural alliances is even more challenging. In today's global environment, it is essential that entrepreneurs begin to look outside of their immediate communities for partners and alliances. Even in the realm of small businesses, cross-cultural alliances can be made.

The greatest difference that I found was that other cultures, outside of the Western cultures, have a greater tendency to partner and support their comrades. While these cultures support one another more aggressively, they also have their share of charlatans and unscrupulous business people. They have similar barriers to accessing capital from mainstream capital markets and have been resourceful at developing their own financing entities.

I have found that if you present yourself and your business in a professional manner, almost anyone will be willing to work with you, and those who do not work with you because of cultural differences would have proved to create poor business relationships anyway.

## *Exiting a failed partnership*

So, what happens when the partnership doesn't work? I have heard more stories than I care to remember about failed partnerships. In the beginning, the partnership always seems like a great idea. A partnership seems like a better idea than going it alone. After all, isn't it better to split the work and responsibility? Isn't it always better when you can have someone help you toe the line so to speak? Not always.

Partnerships can fail for any number of reasons. There could be a disagreement on the way the business is being operated. There could be a change in one of the partner's family structure. One partner could relocate geographically. One partner could be mishandling funds. Or perhaps a partner is not giving his all to increase the sales of the business. Whatever the reason, if things have gotten to the point that the partnership no longer works, how do you get out?

If no major money has been invested in the startup, and if it is early in the partnership and the business hasn't generated a significant amount of revenue, and if there are no savings or reserves to split, then the decision to exit a partnership becomes easy. No harm, no foul, as they say. But if there have been major investments and profits made, things become a little trickier. This is where it is important that you have already documented how the partnership will be handled in the event of dissolution. You can't wait until it's time to leave to figure out how you're going to address all the issues that come when a partnership is done.

If you do not have a document in place and your business has significant assets to dispose of, chances are it will be difficult to exit the partnership unless both partners are in total agreement about how the business closure will be addressed.

One of the ways to address a failed partnership is to have an option in the organizational documents that gives both partners the "right of first refusal." This means that if one partner decides for whatever reason that he or she want to leave the firm, the other partner could buy the exiting partner's interest in a pre-agreed-upon method. The document should also address what will happen to a partner's business interest in the event of death. Finally, the agreement should address how disputes and discrepancies within the partnership will be decided if the partners cannot agree upon a solution. One of the best, least expensive ways to settle potentially litigious situations is to use a mediator or arbitrator before engaging the court system. A mediator is licensed to help mediate disputes. Generally, the mediator is an independent person who has no interest in either partner's outcome.

## ☼ Success Secrets

No one would argue that two people can usually work better and do more than one. But for that to be true, both people must agree to be on the same page. If not, two people can end up doing less than one.

Partnerships can be a great way to accelerate your business and share the work load, but they must be entered carefully and with great consideration. I have seen people get out of marriages easier than getting out of business partnerships, and for less money.

So, choose your partner wisely!

# Chapter 7

## Nine essential mindsets for entrepreneurial success

*"Excellence is an art won by training and habituation. We do not act rightly because we have virtue or excellence, but we rather have those because we have acted rightly. We are what we repeatedly do. Excellence, then, is not an act but a habit."*

*- Aristotle*

## Three Things to Think About

1. Habits and the way that we think, more than anything, are what govern our lives. Yet we give little time to developing good ones. To be successful in entrepreneurship you must develop good habits and ways of thinking.

2. When starting a business, in the beginning you should be willing to do things that others won't, so that in the future you can live a life that others can't.

3. Entrepreneurship doesn't end once the business has been started, you still must continue to develop yourself and your business acumen.

As an entrepreneur and small business owner, it is essential that you accept the responsibility of leadership. As the owner of a business, you are responsible for managing the day-to-day affairs of your business at every level. Even if you can have employees who work for you, it will still be necessary for you to manage them and inspect what you expect. It is not enough to place expectations on those who work for you. It is always necessary that you follow up and ensure that your employees are doing things the way that they are intended to be done.

And as the business owner responsibility for all aspects of the business fall on you. Everything from how to find funding, paying expenses, hiring employees, dealing with clients and the list goes on.

So, to exhibit the type of leadership and responsibility necessary, it will be necessary that you develop some core mindsets or characteristics. Some of these you may have and some of them you may not. But if you want to be successful you must develop all of them.

## 1. Beg, borrow, or steal

This is an old adage that can be applied directly to your entrepreneurial endeavor. While I do not condone the literal meaning of steal, this phrase suggests that you do whatever it takes to accomplish your goal. The primary principle of business is to stay in business. As long as the doors are open, to your physical or virtual business, you always have a chance at success. So, it is essential that you be prepared to do whatever it takes legally and ethically to keep your doors open.

At some point, you may have to do some version of all three of these. In the early stages, you may have to beg or humbly ask for funding, clients, referrals, support and even employees. I can recall several instances in my own past where I have had to borrow money from friends and family. There have been several instances when I had employees who I had to ask to wait a few days before they received their check. While this was not a comfortable feeling, I had no choice.

In entrepreneurship, you have to swallow your pride and do what it takes to keep your business open. I keep going back to the analogy of your business being like a baby. What would a parent do to keep his or her child fed and healthy? Almost anything.

## 2. *Cash is king*

In the last chapter, we said that money isn't everything; but this statement should be taken in context. In terms of maintaining a viable business cash flow is king, money is everything. Cash flow is the lifeblood of any business. Without money, a business cannot grow. Bartering, bootstrapping, and crowdfunding are all effective sources of start-up funds. But as your business progresses, you should be focused on making a profit. You should take your profits, reinvest some, and save others.

You should be keenly focused on making as much money possible without compromising your values or sacrificing the quality of your product or service. Bartering and such are great but, in many instances, nothing speaks louder than cold hard cash.

## 3. *Networking, sales, and marketing*

The best advice that I have to offer entrepreneurs who are trying to grow their businesses is to do what our parents always told us never to do: talk to strangers. In my opinion, the skill that is most essential for successful entrepreneurship is the ability to engage in successful networking, sales, and marketing. The key to any successful business, particularly a start-up business, is to gain quick market presence and exposure. This means that, in a short amount of time, as many people as possible should be able to learn about your business. The only way for this to happen is for you or someone on your team to tell them about it. You can tell that story one-on-one, or you can tell that story using advertising media, such as printed collateral, broadcast media, or online media.

To be successful in business, you need to be a people person to some degree. Now, that doesn't mean that you have to be the extroverted, gregarious type. It does mean that you cannot be afraid to talk with other people about your business and about your ideas. You can't be afraid to speak with people about your business.

## 4. *Destroy preconceived notions and cultural biases*
Another important thing that you must do is to destroy any preconceived notions or cultural biases that you have about your business and the market you hope to service. You must always be open to new opportunities and ideas for your business. Successful businesses often go through several iterations of their model before they find one that satisfies their customer base and their own personal interests.

To do this, you must always have an open mind to interact with people without regard to culture, ethnicity, gender, background, or sexual orientation. To make assumptions that a particular group of people will or will not patronize your business based on prejudiced ideology will negatively impact your business. Use demographic information to assist you in defining your target market(s), but once you have found your target market, do not discount the possibility that there are other segments of the population that are potential customers, as well.

## 5. *No risk, no reward*
No risk, no reward is a very old concept that is typically applied to the investment community. It means that if you are not willing to risk anything, then it is highly unlikely that you will receive any significant return. This is true in every aspect of our regular lives. For instance, if

you are in a romantic relationship, you have to risk your feelings to receive the benefits of romantic love.

If you have ever participated in any sort of athletic contest, you had to take the risk of losing to have the reward of being the victor. If you have been involved in a political campaign, you had to take the risk of losing time and money to receive the reward of being the winning candidate. The same is true in entrepreneurship and business. You must take some risks, and there's no way to guarantee that you will be successful. One thing is for sure: if you do not take the risk, you will not be successful.

## 6. *Receiving wise counsel*

Having a team of trusted advisors and counselors is one of the most important things that any aspiring entrepreneur can do. If you were to ask many entrepreneurs about how they learned about successful entrepreneurship, they would tell you that they learned it from other entrepreneurs. Much of what you will learn as an entrepreneur will not come from formal education, classes, or workshops. It will come from entrepreneurs and small business owners who have lived and breathed entrepreneurship. There is no substitute for experience.

The sooner you surround yourself with a competent team of advisors, the sooner you will move toward success. When selecting your team, be sure to take steps to ensure that your team is diverse in terms of age, gender, cultural background, and industry. Getting different perspectives on your product or service will only make it stronger. Don't have only advisors that are in your specific industry or field. You want people around you who will help you think and see things differently.

## 7. *Personal development equals profits*

Once you have gotten your counselors and advisors in place, always make time to educate and develop yourself and your skills. The market is constantly changing. As an entrepreneur, you must keep up. Many once-thriving businesses are no longer around because the ownership failed to innovate. Do you remember Blockbuster Video? How about America Online (AOL)? What happened to them?

Invest in educating yourself on specific skills, such as computer applications and other technology, writing, and public speaking. Develop soft skills as well, such as networking, interpersonal relationships, and employee management.

In fact, as your business grows, your networking and people skills also should grow. More business usually means more customers, clients, and employees. These mean more people and more relationships.

## 8. *Eat what you kill*

Rarely do business opportunities involve simply picking them up off the ground. You've heard it said that money doesn't grow on trees. Business opportunities don't either. Identify the opportunities you should aggressively pursue. In entrepreneurship, there is no paycheck every two weeks. If you do not make the revenue needed to support your business, that means no paycheck. So, the common saying in entrepreneurship is that you eat what you kill. If you do not identify and take advantage of opportunities, then you won't eat – literally or figuratively.

Not only will you not eat but it is possible that your family and your employees, if you have any, may not eat either. Shouldering the responsibility of having others depend on you and your business for their livelihood can be daunting. When you own a business, you must constantly hunt for new opportunities. You, your family, and your business never stop needing to eat.

## 9. *Realistic expectations*

Entrepreneurs are some of the most optimistic people on the planet. In fact, entrepreneurs are generally overly optimistic. We typically see the glass as half full and we generally see the proverbial silver lining in every cloud, even in the midst of a tornado. So, it is difficult for entrepreneurs to rein in their overly optimistic attitudes and create realistic expectations for themselves and their businesses.

Setting realistic expectations does not mean that you must sacrifice your desire to dream big. After all, it is those big dreams that brought you to this point. Maintaining realistic expectations simply means that you look at the resources you have and look at where you want your business to go. Then you plan regarding how to get there the most efficient way possible. For instance, it is probably somewhat unrealistic for you to believe that you will have your own multi-million-dollar company by the end of the year if you have no money in the bank and haven't even started the business yet.

However, it is realistic to say that if you have one thousand dollars in the bank, you can begin the necessary paperwork to start your business. Once you start your business and have five thousand dollars or so in profits, you can then say that you have the resources to add additional business capacity. And then when the company has revenues of one hundred thousand dollars, you might be able to hire a part-time salesperson.

When you have a part-time salesperson, your revenues might grow to two hundred fifty thousand dollars, which would allow you to hire an additional production person to keep up with demand. With yourself, a salesperson, and an additional production person, revenues could grow to five hundred thousand dollars.

With revenues at five hundred thousand dollars, you might have enough money to hire another salesperson. You would then have yourself, two salespeople, and additional production people, allowing your company to grow from revenues of five hundred thousand dollars to 1.5 million dollars.

This whole process might take three to five years, which is more realistic than expecting to go from nothing to 1.5 million dollars in one year. I am never one to say that something is not possible, but it isn't probable for start-ups to see this type of success. Even Facebook went through several years of no revenue before they received the billion-dollar blow-up opportunity.

## ☼ Success Secrets

Acquiring the above-mentioned mindsets is essential to successful entrepreneurship. What you do, how you do it, and how often you do it is important. When you start your own business, there is no supervisor to tell you what to do. No one will tell you to work harder or do better. You must have personal motivation to be successful. You should have developed the habits and mindsets that will allow you to effortlessly make the right decisions at the right times.

It is not enough to have a few of the above listed traits, you must have them all. If you do not have all the traits, the good news is that you can learn them. You just have to put forth the effort.

# Chapter 8
## Failure is Feedback

*"Far better is it to dare mighty things, to win glorious triumphs, even though checkered by failure ... than to rank with those poor spirits who neither enjoy nor suffer much, because they live in a gray twilight that knows not victory nor defeat."*

*-Theodore Roosevelt*

---

### Three Things to Think About

1. Only people who never try never fail. If you are reading this book, you have made the decision to try.

2. Business failure is the market's way of telling you to simply try your business or idea again but a different way.

3. People aren't failures, ever! People sometimes fail at accomplishing the things that they want out to do, but there is a big difference between the two.

## *Failure is a precursor to success*

Just saying the "F" word "failure" invokes all sort of negative emotions. But the real definition is not that frightening at all. According to Wikipedia: "**Failure** is the state or condition of not meeting a desirable or intended objective." If the definition of failure is so simple, why do we attach so many additional connotations to the word?

I am a strong believer that as entrepreneurs we should be more transparent about our successes and failures in life in order to provide realistic examples of what it means to be successful or to fail. Sometimes I feel that we have exalt entrepreneurship and turned it into some mystical endeavor. I am a strong critique of those successful entrepreneurs that glorify and recount their stories of success and building million dollar companies, all seemingly with great ease, or so they would have us believe, believe that it is an opportunity to make millions of dollars in record time with ground-breaking technical apps and inventions. Nothing could be further from the truth.

My first big failure in business came when I was 31-years old, married for about a year, living in a new home and had a newborn. I had a couple failures prior to this time, but none with the level of financial and emotional repercussions of this one. I had opened my first restaurant and after only a year or so I was out of business. I had borrowed money against our new home, opened credit accounts for restaurant equipment, and I owed the landlord six months of rent. In total I had spent close to $100,000 and was still in debt for around $65,000. I had no money, no job and no credit.

One evening around 7:00pm my wife Dionne and I, along with our newborn daughter, Kayla were sitting at home about to eat dinner. Suddenly we heard a loud and startling knock at the front door. I peered through the window blinds and looked outside and saw a police car, a county sheriff's car to be more exact. Apprehensively I approached the door and asked, "who is it", as if I didn't know. To which the officer replied Officer Williams with the Sheriff's Department. I opened the door and the Sherriff's deputy asked if I was Kevin McGee. I answered yes and he proceeded to give me a legal summons. My lender had sued me for defaulting on a business loan. Unfortunately, this was the first business-related summons I received, but it would not be the last.

So, at the ripe old age of 31 I had my first series of business litigations. By the time it was over, I was sued more than seven times by seven different creditors. By the time I hit 33, I had been involved in more lawsuits, mediations, and consent agreements than most people will ever be a part of in their entire lives. I considered myself a professional at the art of dispute resolution. I learned very quickly what attorneys could and could not do in the realm of business law. I knew exactly how long it could take to sue a business owner, get a judgment and try to begin collection efforts. In the beginning, the Sheriff knocking on the door to serve the summons was a little unnerving but it eventually became normal for me and I would even offer them a bottle of water on particularly hot days.

So, here I was newly married with no business, no money, and a young child. The next three years of my life were one of the darkest times I've ever experienced. I was happy to be married and to have a child, but the stress owing so much money from the restaurant failure was tremendous. I had pledged my home as collateral for the loan that I used to start the restaurant. So, now I had the stress of not knowing whether my family would be able to continue living in our home. It was hard. I had no job and no work history for the last couple of years when I ran the restaurant, and consequently no income for several months.

Failing at something and losing a lot of money can make you feel inadequate. After all the hoopla with opening my restaurant, I was embarrassed by the failure. I was ashamed to go out with friends and often went the other way when I saw people that I knew. I felt like everyone was looking at me and laughing. Now I know that these perceptions were just my own and more a matter of personal insecurities. I wondered what my next steps would be, and I walked around with my head held low for several years after the restaurant failed. It took 3 years before we straightened out all the financial consequences. But we did it.

I quickly began to understand that failure is life's form of feedback. And as is the case with most people I was not inclined to hear feedback and criticism of my performance. I had no appreciation for failure. It's odd that something so common in our lives experienced since birth, still is so loathed. We have all failed at something in our lives perhaps numerous times. Even our first steps as babies came after dozens of attempts and falls. But we obviously kept getting up.

Very early in my entrepreneurial career, I became comfortable with failure. I quickly began to understand that failure is just life's feedback. Most of us are not inclined to receive criticism, and so we don't often appreciate the lessons we can learn from failure. We have all failed at something in our lives. Even our first walking steps as babies came after dozens of attempts and falls. But we kept getting up, though.

People focus heavily on the anomalies of successful entrepreneurship. When most people think of successful entrepreneurs, they think of Bill Gates, Steve Jobs, Oprah Winfrey, Robert Johnson, or maybe John D. Rockefeller or Ted Turner. We always seem to associate entrepreneurship with people who have made millions – if not billions of dollars. But every successful entrepreneur that has ever lived has failed at some point in their journey of being an entrepreneurship. If you find an entrepreneur that says they have never failed, they are lying. Let me end this section with a few little-known examples.

Let's start with the richest man in the world, Bill Gates.

**Bill Gates** dropped out of Harvard and his first failed venture was a business he started with Microsoft co-founder Paul Allen called Traf-O-Data, which failed horribly. You have never even heard of it. But Gates didn't quit. And look at him now.

**Soichiro Honda:** The billion-dollar business that is Honda began with a series of failures and fortunate turns of luck. Honda was turned down by Toyota Motor Corporation for a job after interviewing for a job as an engineer, leaving him jobless for quite some time. He started making scooters of his own at home, and spurred on by his neighbors, finally started his own business.

**Oprah Winfrey**: The first African-American Woman Billionaire was not always destined for success. In fact, many might say that she was destined for failure looking at her early life. She started in one of the poorest communities in America. She was born in rural Mississippi in the 1950's to a teenage mother. She was physically and sexually abused from the age of 9-years old, ran away at 13-years old, became pregnant at 14-years old and lost her baby shortly after birth. Yet she pushed through all of that to be where she is today.

**Akio Morita:** You may not have heard of Morita but you've undoubtedly heard of his company, Sony. Sony's first product was a rice cooker that unfortunately didn't cook rice so much as burn it, selling less than 100 units. This first setback didn't stop Morita and his partners as they pushed forward to create what would ultimately become SONY, a multi-billion-dollar company.

**Walt Disney:** Who hasn't heard of Walt Disney? Today Disney makes billions of dollars from merchandise, theme parks, movies, and other ventures. But Walt Disney was fired from one of his earlier jobs at a newspaper because, "he lacked imagination and had no good ideas." After this Disney tried a number of businesses that all failed and eventually ended up in bankruptcy. But he kept at it and learned from his mistakes.

**Harland David Sanders:** Perhaps better known as Colonel Sanders of Kentucky Fried Chicken fame, Sanders had a hard time selling his chicken at first. In fact, his famous secret chicken recipe was rejected 1,009 times before a restaurant accepted it. And after that he continued to work through challenges before becoming the household name it is today.

Some might say that these billionaire entrepreneurs are the exception and not the rule. But are they really? Could it be that they turned failure into fuel that would move their entrepreneurial dreams forward? Do they have a set of habits, traits and behaviors that have allowed them to be successful? Do they take care of and pay attention to their minds, bodies and souls? It is a widely held notion that success and successful people leave clues. We just have to look at them and use them to find our way to success. Not only in entrepreneurship but in life.

### *Entrepreneurship and corporate America*
As an entrepreneur and businessman, I have experienced both corporate and entrepreneurial environments. The corporate environments seem to offer more security and sense of status in terms of earning power and job titles. But there are many requirements that accompany this earning power and corporate status. Often an unreasonable commitment of time and energy is required for these corporate careers. This corporate commitment is not always reciprocal, though. Corporations are infamous for laying off or transitioning lifelong employees with little thought or consideration.

Over the last twenty-five years, I have had at least twenty-five different hourly or salaried jobs. Many of them were only guises so that I could earn enough money to start another business. Fortunately – or unfortunately, depending on your perspective – almost all of these hourly and corporate jobs ended with me saying, "I quit" or with me being fired. Name an industry, and I can almost guarantee that I have worked in it: financial services, insurance, food service, clothing, retail, telemarketing – you name it, and I have done it. One summer, I even sold encyclopedias door-to-door. Some of you reading this book may not even know what an encyclopedia is. It was the worst job ever.

I have also started and closed more businesses than I care to remember. There have been at least six or seven formal business entities and dozens of business ideas ("side hustles," you might call them) that I have started. One thing I have learned is that entrepreneurship is hard work, and to be successful, you must be committed to it and constantly willing to learn and adjust to changing markets. In the end, the benefits of entrepreneurship far outweigh the challenges.

### *Learn something from everything that you do*
Entrepreneurship at its best occurs when a person has the courage and conviction to pursue his or her passion and God's calling upon their lives. After you have the courage and conviction to start a business, you must have the fortitude to keep going. It is almost a certainty that your first business venture will not go as planned. According to Bloomberg Statistics, eight out of ten businesses fail within the first few two years of starting. In other words, if you were in a room with nine other business owners, eight of you would be out of business within a few years. Most of us think that ours will be the two businesses out of ten to beat the odds. We can't all be right.

Entrepreneurship is a lifelong journey – not a destination. If you look at some of the most accomplished contemporary entrepreneurs, you will see that their early lives were full of failed attempts, missed opportunities, and just plain old screw ups. They learned from their mistakes, though, improved on their concepts, and kept at it.

Entrepreneurship is just as much about endurance as it is invention. Failure is a crucial part of success for virtually every type of inventive activity, which is at the heart of entrepreneurship. Even in science, researchers find new cures, inventions, or protocols by trying to achieve a certain outcome and ruling out what did not work. When you rule out what doesn't work, you are left with what does work.

Even though he did not invent the light bulb per se, it's rumored that Thomas Edison created thousands of versions of the light bulb's design before finding the one that worked. Bill Gates and Steve Jobs both created hundreds, if not thousands, of failed algorithms and programs before coming up with Microsoft's and Apple's operating systems. It is important to learn something from everything that you do. It is not enough to just go through entrepreneurial endeavors for the sake of it. Learn from your failures as much as you would from your successes.

### Prepare for the inevitable
I am no pessimist. I am quite the opposite. If I see a glass holding even a small amount of water, it looks half full to me. I am the epitome of overly optimistic. Over the years, that outlook has cost me a great deal of mental, physical, emotional, and financial anguish. Nevertheless, I wouldn't change for anything.

What I *would* change is to make sure that I prepared myself more for the inevitability of failure. It is possible to be optimistic while still taking proper precautions. Many entrepreneurs bet the house on that one big idea or one big venture – and sometimes they lose it all.

That's why it's important to go into your venture with your eyes wide open and prepared for whatever may happen. You need to emotionally, mentally and financially ready yourself and your family for the possibility of failure.

## Build your confidence and strengthen your resolve

You must work on building your self-confidence if you want to be successful in entrepreneurship. There will be very few people there to truly cheer you on. Very few will say, "Hey, go out there and start that business, risk your livelihood, enjoy the stress and strain." However, there will be lots of people around once you are successful. They will ask you for your advice and for your business to sponsor the school soccer club. And you will become the de facto financier for your immediate and extended family's financial shortcomings and needs.

Building confidence before success is essential. You must have faith in your product and faith in yourself. If you're not confident about your business, no one else will be. People can sense when you are not confident, almost like wild animals sense fear. To quote one of my favorite historical figures, Sun Tzu, "When you are weak you should appear as though you are strong." You should stand with your entrepreneurial chest out at all times.

I have found three ways that to best build self-confidence. The first is to surround yourself with like-minded people. The easiest way to do this is to join an entrepreneurial or small business group – not to generate business, but for support. The second is to listen to motivational speakers in your field who have done what you are trying to do. Their words and accounts of their journeys will be food to your soul. Finally, try to invest in personal development opportunities for yourself. These might include attending conferences, taking courses, or earning industry certifications.

Building your confidence and strengthening your resolve will help you greatly in dealing with failure. Trust me when I say this, you are going to fail. You may not want to hear it, but you need to listen to me. I will say it again, you are going to fail. So, if you know and believe that then you need to prepare for it. Just like when you took those first steps as a baby, you fell but your desire to walk was greater than your desire to stay down. So, when you fail, don't stay down, get back, shake it off and try again.

## ☼ Success Secrets

Failure is something that everyone has experienced in one form or another. It is a precursor to every success that we have and it is essential to learning. When we were babes, we learned to walk after numerous attempts that resulted in us falling down. The fact that you are walking today means that you were determined enough to get back up and try again.

It's the same in business. Yes, the stakes are a little higher with business failure, but the notion of getting back up and continuing to try, still rings true. That's why it is so important that you assess if you have the personality and fortitude to keep getting up and keep trying when you fail. If you can, the rewards of successful entrepreneurship can be you

# Chapter 9

## Taking the first steps toward starting your business

*"The hardest part of any journey is taking the first step"*

- *Unknown*

### Three Things to Think About

1. The biggest killer of entrepreneurial dreams and aspirations is procrastination.

2. Entrepreneurship is not just whimsical notion. It takes a lot of hard work. Sometimes you may or may not have what it takes to survive. You must be prepared.

3. Just like when you were a baby, taking those first steps can be scary. But you must do it or you will be sitting on your butt forever.

## *Start now*

You don't have to wait until you have the perfect situation to start your business. You can start now, regardless of where you are. This doesn't mean that I am suggesting you go out tomorrow and get a loan, lease a space, buy inventory, or do anything to physically start your business. What I am saying is that you should use your time wisely and start working on your business now. There is always something you can be doing to grow your business.

By this I mean that it doesn't cost anything to go online and research your business ideas. You could begin working on your business concept or even your website. You could start testing out your product or service ideas on family and friends. You could start attending classes and learning more about your industry.

Don't believe that since you do not have five hundred thousand dollars in venture capital that you cannot start your business. Nor should you believe that you necessarily need that much to start. I am happy that there are several reality shows that discuss various aspects of entrepreneurship. The shows have brought much-needed attention to the trials and tribulations of being an entrepreneur. But inadvertently what some of the shows have done is to create an unrealistic image of what an entrepreneur really is.

As a result, many entrepreneurs feel that they have to start out their businesses with all the bells and whistles and often put everything they have on the line to get going. Instead, what these entrepreneurs should do is look at what capital they have available to invest. Next, they should determine what would be the best version of their business if they started now. Remember that you don't need to wait until everything is in place. The true definition of success is when preparation meets opportunity. And your goal as an entrepreneur is to be prepared to the fullest.

So, when you see iconic figures on shows listening to million-dollar pitches from entrepreneurs, you may think that your small idea doesn't have a place. That is most not true. As I mentioned earlier, everyone has something to contribute to this entrepreneur ecosystem, and the best thing that you can do is to start exactly where you are.

In fact, many of these multi-millionaires received a head start from a family-owned business. I don't mean to suggest that it's wrong to take advantage of your family legacy. A person would be crazy not to leverage what their family has built. What I am saying is that you, as a start-up entrepreneur, you should not try to compare yourself to these individuals. It is not a fair comparison.

Your personal preparation is the only factor you can truly control. Opportunity is rarely a controllable factor. You can seldom engineer being in the right place at the right time. But you can make sure that you are prepared all the time.

## *Procrastination*
Why do we procrastinate? Are our reasons legitimate? Demands from our family, careers, and personal interests are all things that can lead to delaying our goal to start a business; but, there will always be reasons not to start.

There are any number of things that you can work on right now as it pertains to your business, regardless of where you stand. If you are in the planning stages and working a full-time job while you prepare, you can gather market data and research about your industry. If you are in your senior year of college and want to start a company, you can form relationships with classmates and colleagues who can help you with your business. If you are working a part-time job in your desired industry, you can begin to identify suppliers, vendors, and competitors.

Procrastination is the biggest enemy of success. How many times have you made plans to engage in a new hobby or set a new goal only to look up years later and see that you have made no progress?

One major advantage to starting now is that you force yourself to constantly work on your business, and this keeps it in the forefront of your mind. Imagine if some of the greatest entrepreneurs and inventors of all time had never reached their full potential? What if Bill Gates never started Microsoft? What if it had just languished as a business plan? The world might be a much different place. As an entrepreneur, there is something that you are intended to provide to the world, so procrastination is not an option. Avoid depression and self-pity by starting now. Do something.

### *Create a plan and set a timeline*

The most important step in starting a business is to create a plan of action complete with timelines and deadlines. If you do not create a plan and implement it, nothing will ever happen. If you have the bad habits like procrastination, laziness, or being easily discouraged, you may not be ready for entrepreneurship. There will surely be times that you will feel discouraged, times that you need to be driven, and times that you think about giving up. You must have the fortitude to be able to push through. And, until you become a person with fortitude and drive, trying to become an entrepreneur is an exercise in futility. Know who you are.

There are three key considerations when creating your plan. The first is to know specifically what you want to do. The second is when is the right time. And the third is where do you want to be located.

## *What type of business should you start?*

The rule of thumb in entrepreneurship is to do what you love. But it has been my experience that some people don't know exactly what they love to do. Rather, they know what they are good at doing. The two are very different.

One of my businesses was a restaurant management company. For more than a decade, I opened and operated any number of independent restaurants and franchises. I found that I was very good at this and had an almost instinctive knowledge of food and food culture. And this was before Food Network, *Top Chef*, and *Chopped*. I had even managed to achieve the coveted position of a certified executive chef.

My background up until this point had largely been a business consulting and financial
background. There was really nothing in my past to indicate that I would own and operate a successful restaurant company, much less become an executive chef.

As my time in that career wound down, I found myself feeling burned out, and I took an extended break. Now, when the opportunities come to provide services for people, I am still somewhat reluctant. I remember the long, hard days I spent as an entrepreneur and executive chef, and the pain comes rushing back to me.

I have learned that you must be careful when deciding what business to go into. You should analyze what it is you think you want to do. Spend a lot of time speaking to other people in the field of interest. You might find that the core of the business is not at all what you thought. I was not interested in the day-to-day operation of a restaurant or food service company. It was what I had to do to survive. I found that I loved to create restaurant concepts and culinary menus, but that had no real interest in the development and operation of the business after concept. I was only interested again when it was time to address a particular problem that required a unique solution. It took me ten years to find out that I didn't love all aspects of the industry. So, instead of starting a company that started and operated restaurants, I should have started a company that provided creative services for restaurant build-outs. Or maybe even a company that dealt with menu creation and training.

Take a close look at your skill set and compare it to your passion. You don't have to love what you do to be successful at it. I've heard people debate whether you should do something you love or make yourself love what you do. I think the old saying goes, "If you can't be with the one you love, love the one you're with." For entrepreneurship, I think that this is partly true.

A great deal depends upon your personal financial situation. Plainly put, money can "buy" patience and help ease some of the burdens you might have engaging in some businesses. If you currently have a job or another source of income and your small business will just be another stream of income, I would say yes, you might look at businesses that you don't love but that have good returns. In life, one thing I have learned is that you must have areas in your life in which you feel fulfilled and in control. If you are happy with your job, you do not have to be as happy with your side business.

However, if you are not happy at your job and are not happy with your home life, then you must, at all costs, be happy with the business that you operate. If you are not, then what's the point? If you decide to engage in a business while you have another stream of income, that's great. While you may not necessarily be in love with the business that you are operating, you will find comfort in the fact that you are making additional income that you can one day use to do the things you really want to do.

By contrast, if you are starting a business out of some necessity, i.e. you were downsized and have not been able to find employment, a divorce or other situation has put you in a predicament, or if you decided to just take the plunge and go for it full time, that's a different story. In this case, you want to start a business that you get some enjoyment out of, because you might be doing this business day and night until you have reached a break-even point.

Your passion for your product will be evident when you are out in the market making sales calls to your potential clients. If you do not have this love for your business or have been burned out prematurely, your customers and clients won't see the great idea. They will see an overworked employee who does not appear to believe in what he or she is selling. If you have the perfect situation, and you have outside income *and* you love what you do, you are in a great position. Your love for your craft combined with your financial stability will take you far.

Consider Thomas, a good friend of mine who owns a gourmet hot dog business. This guy has turned hot dogs into a multi-million-dollar business. Thomas comes from a very successful family and went to an Ivy League university to earn his MBA.

Those academic pursuits were solely to satisfy his parents. Thomas's real love was cooking. He spent much of his time in college and grad school cooking for friends at parties and fraternity houses. The main staple of many of these parties was grilled hot dogs and burgers. Thomas developed his own line of creative culinary concoctions that became cult favorites in the college scene.

Much to the dismay of his parents, Thomas did not go to work for a Fortune 500 company when he finished grad school. Instead, he started a hot dog stand on a busy street corner in Atlanta. It wasn't exactly what his parents expected after investing more than one hundred thousand dollars into his education.

But Thomas was adamant about pursuing his passion. The first year, he did not do very well, as you may imagine. The market for food in Atlanta is fairly saturated. Also, Atlanta is not as pedestrian friendly and dense other metropolises, like New York City. Selling hot dogs on the corner is difficult. But Thomas was not deterred. His parents were still pretty upset with him, but they provided him with food and a place to stay. As a twenty-five-year-old, he didn't need much else.

What his parents began to see was that Thomas was diligent about what he wanted to do. Every day, he would get up at six in the morning and begin the routine of preparing his cart, purchasing food items, and making marketing calls. And when his day was over at six o'clock in the evening, he would come home, eat dinner, and begin his evening ritual of counting the day's receipts, unpacking his cart, meticulously cleaning it, and organizing for the next day. Thomas did this six days a week and worked at it for twelve to thirteen hours each day.

What amazed his parents was that he did all of this with no complaints. His parents could not remember a time that Thomas had ever routinely gotten up early and worked late. They never recalled him taking such interest in a particular thing. His mother, on occasion, would even give him money to go out with his friends and have a good time. But Thomas would take the money and invest it in his cart, and was happy to sit at home by himself and watch TV. Having lived a pretty privileged life, it was even hurtful to his parents at times to see their son "suffering."

Even his friends were beginning to question his sanity. Thomas's classmates had successful careers, were living in midtown condos, driving BMWs, and partying regularly on the weekends. Thomas was selling hot dogs on the corner.

After about a year, Thomas was still at it and was still unwavering in his commitment. He had many regular clients, and his popularity began to grow in the downtown area. He even began to have lines of people waiting for his gourmet hot dogs and hamburgers. Thomas's passion for his business was so infectious that eventually his parents, who had the means, decided to support him.

With a twenty-five thousand-dollar loan, Thomas was able to secure a small, fixed location inside a busy office building. All he had to do was make some minor renovations, and he was open for business.

Thomas had no major costs to outfit a kitchen, grill, or excessive refrigeration. He had a lean and clean business model. So, with this investment, he prepaid his rent and was able to get a ten percent discount. He purchased marketing materials, flyers, and business cards. He even found a local bike messenger company that was willing to take a small fee to deliver his gourmet hotdogs. Within a matter of months, Thomas's business was taking off. His experience in college and his MBA were invaluable as he began to manage the growth of his company.

He was able to chart his growth, make financial projections, and package his concept. Within another year, he began to locate other buildings that he felt would be great locations for his concept. Within a few months of opening each, he would locate franchisees or owner operators to take over the reins. Within five years, he had more than ten locations and had combined sales in excess of three million dollars per year. From selling hotdogs. Eventually, Thomas exited the business, sold the stores, and made a pretty penny. He took his cash and opened a full-service restaurant and bar and is now one of the premier restaurateurs in Atlanta. But it all started with selling hot dogs.

## *When is the right time for entrepreneurship?*
Maybe you want to start your business as soon as you graduate college. But is that the right time? If you have graduated, have student loan debt, credit card debt, and have yet to make any income, is that really the best time to start a business? What about if you're an adult who has just had a child and must spend time helping your spouse parent? Is that really the best time to start a business?

Only you can answer that question. Don't make an emotional decision, though. The right business at the wrong time will always fail. A lot of people romanticize entrepreneurship. Starting a business should not be a knee-jerk reaction. It should only be the result of significant planning and preparation. You should be stable if you want to be successful at entrepreneurship.

(Remember that starting doesn't mean that you have to jump right in. It could mean that you begin the data-gathering process.)

Speaking a little more about financial readiness, you really need to be able to withstand the risks related to starting a business. That means that your personal financial situation should be stable so that you can focus your energy on your business and not your personal financial issues.

For example, it may be a little hard for you to focus on growing your business when you're worried about whether your checks can be garnished. Or if you are worried about whether you will have money to pay your rent. Or if you're worried about not being able to make your minimum credit card payment. You absolutely must have some way to support your personal expenses when you start your business. The notion that you can give up everything you have and do whatever it takes (including sleep in the car or eating ramen noodles and peanuts for every meal) and one day be a millionaire is more fantasy that fact.

My advice for you would be to begin to save to finance your business venture. And, while you're saving, continue to work on planning your strategy for success. You may have to work a few years to save money and prepare like I did. But, in the end, you stand a better chance of being successful. You must be strategic about when to start your business.

## *Where will your business be located?*

Who, what, when, and now *where*. When I started my business, the *where* was pretty simple: Atlanta. Today, though, the *where* is limitless. Because of the proliferation of the Internet, you could start a business virtually anywhere. Through online commerce, you can be in Atlanta and sell your products or services in Ireland. Geography no longer plays as much of a role in starting and maintaining a business as it did in the past.

As you think about your business, where you will start is a tough question, because you have so many options. Do you want a storefront? Do you want to sell online? Do you want to sell via mobile office? Own the one-operator food truck? Or do you want to operate a brick-and-mortar restaurant? The *where* is important.

Also, you must decide where you want to make an impact. Do you want to impact your local community? Do you want to impact your region? Or do you want to impact the world? Where you want to make your impact will greatly affect where you want to establish your business. Where's your niche, and where is your target? You must have the right location to be successful, whether that's a physical location or virtual location. A great idea with the wrong location will almost always fail.

You should create a realistic plan and write it down. If the idea in your head doesn't make it to paper, or to an iPad or tablet, then it will never come to be. Any venture that you are serious about will require a plan. You don't have to know all the answers about the type of business that you want to start, yet, and you don't have to create a lengthy business plan to begin the process. You do have to have at least some idea of how you plan to get from where you are now to where you want to be and the steps that you need to take to get there.

The key is that the plan must be realistic. It is wise to temper over-optimism with realistic expectations. In almost every start-up situation, it would be unrealistic to assume that the business would make one million dollars in the first year. Yet, many aspiring entrepreneurs have this lofty goal. Have dreams – even seemingly unrealistic ones; but understand what you desire to do and understand, realistically, what you must do to get there.

I also suggest that potential entrepreneurs make some sort of personal assessment of their strengths and weakness and match those to what it takes to be a successful entrepreneur. You must possess or develop the habits of an entrepreneur. Think about your current habits. Much of what you do is based not on what you have been taught, but rather on what you have seen. For the most part, no one has to tell you how to go about your daily routine. And, in general, you probably do many of the same things instinctively. The same is true for many entrepreneurs. Many behaviors should become instinct.

To be successful as an entrepreneur, one of the habits you will have to develop is perseverance. Perseverance means that regardless of what happens, you have the will to push through. Just as important as perseverance is patience. While you're taking your journey to entrepreneurship, things may not happen as quickly as you may like. Exercise patience.

Another key habit to develop is discipline. Do what you said you would do, even when no one is making you do it. Discipline is self-imposed and is crucial to ensuring that you stay on the correct path towards entrepreneurship.

Prepare your lifestyle for the journey of entrepreneurship. The lifestyle of an entrepreneur is very different than that of a person who works nine to five. Shortly after I graduated college, I started a business. I wasn't making very much money, which meant that I didn't really have the money for a lot of the activities that many of my peers enjoyed. Since I was pursuing my business full time and investing every dollar that I made back into it, I had little excess income to wine and dine.

So, if being able to live lavishly and enjoy some of the finer things in life is important to you, entrepreneurship may not be for you. Additionally, the demands on your time when starting a business can be excessive. It's nothing for first time entrepreneurs to spend fifty to sixty hours a week or more working on their businesses. And, in the case of entrepreneurs who work a job while starting their business, it's not uncommon to spend as many as eighty or ninety hours per week between a job and the new business. This leaves little time for other activities.

Finally, consider how you will deal with failure. It is almost inevitable that you will experience some level of failure. You should be prepared to deal with that mentally, emotionally, and financially. It's not how you fall down but how you get up that matters.

# BONUS MATERIAL

## *MAKING YOUR PLAN*

*Below is a bonus of sorts. These are some of the steps that you need to consider when making your plan. There are so many steps that you really can't list them all. But as with the intro quote one step leads to another and another and another. So, review these steps and take them.*

### *Gather market data and research*

One of the easiest things you can do to stay on track with starting your business is to do the research. You can never do enough research on your market niche or general industry. All industries change constantly, and you should be up on all the latest trends in your industry. If you started researching your business several years ago, much of that initial research has changed – and will continue to change. You should begin a process of gathering and collecting business research and ideas. I use a variety of methods to archive vital data and ideas. For those who are tech savvy, there are digital recorders and smart phone apps that can archive your thoughts.

There are also several note-taking and article-clipping software applications that are available to store and archive your data.

### *Identify potential partners and employees*

Another thing you can do is begin the process of identifying people who can help you with the project. These may be potential partners or potential employees, including possible managers, depending on the structure of your business. Bottom line is that no one can start and sustain a business on his or her own.

And if there are not partners or employees in your circle of family and friends, then you should locate small companies or consultants to help. I am talking about more than equity partners. I mean partners such as vendors and suppliers. You can research potential vendors and suppliers and do thorough due diligence to be sure that you are hiring the right people and the right companies.

### *Identify locations, physical or virtual*
You can begin to look for the perfect location for your business. Maybe you need a physical location for your retail business, or maybe it's a virtual location for your Web-based business. (Be mindful that Web-based businesses must be properly positioned in cyberspace to be successful. You can't just put up an e-commerce site and expect people to find it amidst the millions of sites on the Web.)

The rationale is the same for Internet businesses as it is for physical locations. You can't just put your business anywhere. The saying is, "Build it, and they will come." But the truth is, if you build it, they *may* come – depending on where it is located.

### *Networking with potential peers, partners, or customers*
You can also go out into the community and network within your industry. If you are an IT firm, there are several local and national trade groups, associations, and clubs you could join.

Try to begin all your relationships at the local level, and work your way up. There's no need to join the national league of dressmakers when you have not connected with the dressmakers in your city. The local organizations will always have more relevant information to the local environment for your business.

### *Concept Creation*
The most obvious first step is to determine what you want to do. Chances are that you have some idea of what your business should be. If not, spend some time thinking about either what makes you extremely happy or what makes you extremely sad. Put another way:

If helping children learn makes you happy, then seeing children who are illiterate makes you sad. Somewhere in that scenario could be a business that revolves around education, training, tutoring, or resource development.

I often counsel start-up entrepreneurs to think in terms of a broad industry or idea and then refine it to a specific niche, as opposed to the other way around. Sometimes, people have an idea in their head that they just won't let go. And that is ok. But as an entrepreneur, you should always be open to other possibilities.

### Structure
One of the first decisions you must make when starting a business is the type of business you want to create. This decision determines the types of applications you'll need to submit. There are also liability implications for personal investments you make into your business, as well as the taxes you will need to pay.

**Cooperative:** A business or organization that is owned by and operated for the benefit of those using its services. Profits and earnings generated by the cooperative are distributed among the members, also known as user-owners.

**Corporation**: A Corporation is generally suggested for larger established, companies. The annual reporting requirements are excessive for small businesses.

**Limited Liability Corporation (LLC):** A hybrid-type of legal structure that is one of the most popular structures for small businesses because it provides the limited liability features of a corporation with the tax efficiencies and operational flexibility of a partnership. Depending on the state, the members can consist of a single individual (one owner), two or more individuals, corporations, other LLCs, and even other entities. LLCs are not taxed as a separate business entity. Instead, all profits and losses are "passed through" the business to each member of the LLC.

**Partnership:** A single business where two or more people share ownership. Each partner shares in the profits and losses of the business.

**S Corporation:** A special type of corporation created through an IRS tax election. An eligible domestic corporation can avoid double taxation (once to the corporation and again to the shareholders) by electing to be treated as an S corporation.

If you are not comfortable setting up your corporate structure, you should seek legal help. Generally, it can cost between five hundred and fifteen hundred dollars to set up your business, depending on the level of difficulty. In some cases, with adequate research, you can set up your corporate structure on your own.

When considering the type of business structure you'll need, you should always seek legal advice and counsel. If not possible, at a minimum you should get the advice of a reputable business organization like the Small Business Administration.

Quick tip: Regarding legal structure, most small start-ups will be limited liability corporation (LLC) if they are for-profit companies. If you are starting a non-profit, you will have to first form a full-fledged corporation.

## *Show me the money: financing your venture*

The likelihood of your small start-up business receiving a bank loan is slim, unless you already have an abundance of collateral and cash. Then, it would not likely be necessary.

The fact of the matter is there are only a few viable sources of funding. What follows are the possibilities and brief explanations of the sources. You should do more research on all of them and determine the best one for your particular situation.

**Boot strapping**
The oldest form of funding for start-ups. The name is as it implies. You pull yourself and your business up by the boot straps, as they say. Bootstrapping can come in many forms. Some save money while working a full-time job. Some use portions of their retirement accounts or other sources of personal funds.

**Family and friends**
The second most popular option is family and friends. This is still a very good option but, as we mentioned earlier, this could be deemed a partnership of sorts, since it carries the same level of risk in terms of relationship stress. If this is an option, and you have family or friends with the capital to invest, you should be sure to treat it as a business deal, and have firm agreements and understandings in place.

**Bartering**
Bartering is not exactly a way of funding your entire venture, but it is a way to help curtail some of the expenses involved in starting your venture. Depending on your business, you may be able to barter your business's product or service for other useful things such as website design, marketing plans, graphic design, or construction services.

**Crowdfunding**
Although fairly new to many of us, crowdfunding, in its true form, has been around for a while. Essentially, a group of individuals coalesces around a potential venture and provides small amounts of the total amount of funding necessary.

*Private investors*
Private investors are also an option, although not as probable as some of the others that have been discussed. Private investors put equity or cash into a new venture in return for a percentage of ownership. The terms of this option can vary greatly and depend on what the business owner and the investor decide. In general, this is a slightly more difficult option for start-ups. The percentage of ownership that a business has to give up to investors can be steep.

*Micro-loans*
In some cities there are non-profit agencies that operate what are known as micro-loan funds. These are programs that offer smaller loan amounts for start-up and early-stage businesses. Generally, these carry a reasonable interest rate and are tied to some sort of economic development incentive in that city or community.

*Marketing your business*
One of the first steps to business planning is determining your target market and why they would want to buy from you.

For example, is the market you serve the best one for your product or service? Are the benefits of dealing with your business clear, and are they aligned with customer needs? If you are unsure about the answers to any of these questions, take a step back and revisit the foundation of your business plan.

The following tips can help you clarify what your business has to offer, identify the right target market for it, and build a niche for yourself.


Be clear about what you have to offer.

Ask yourself: Beyond basic products or services, what are you really selling? Your town probably has several restaurants, all selling one fundamental product: food. However, each is targeted toward a different need or clientele.

One might be a drive-thru, fast food restaurant, perhaps another sells pizza in a rustic Italian kitchen, and maybe there's a fine-dining seafood restaurant that specializes in wood-grilled fare. All these restaurants sell meals, but they sell them to different clientele who are looking for the unique qualities each has to offer. What they are *really* selling is a combination of product, value, ambience, and brand experience.

When starting a business, be sure to understand what makes your business unique. What needs does your product or service fulfill? What benefits and differentiators will help your business stand out from the crowd?

Don't become a Jack-of-All-Trades – learn to strategize

It's important to clearly define what you're selling. You do not want to become a Jack-of-All-Trades and master of none, because this can have a negative impact on business growth. As a smaller business, it's often a better strategy to divide your products or services into manageable market niches. Small operations can then offer specialized goods and services that are attractive to a specific group of prospective buyers.

Identify your niche

Creating a niche for your business is essential to success. Often, business owners can identify a niche based on their own market knowledge, but it can also be helpful to conduct a market survey with potential customers to uncover untapped needs. During your research process, identify the following:

- In which areas are your competitors already well-established?

- Which areas are being ignored by your competitors?
- Where are the potential opportunities for your business.

## ☼ Success Secrets

The key to starting your business is starting your business. You have to take that first step and start doing something towards making your entrepreneurial dreams a reality. You have to start now!

Perhaps you do not have everything in place, but if you truly want to start, there are things that you can now. You can start planning, researching, and looking for possible lead sources and employees.

You can also start now by creating your plans for financing your venture. You can start raising money from family and friends, saving your own funds, and identifying potential sources of funding so that this is not an issue when it is time to start the business.

Waiting until everything is in place will not help you start a business. In my experience, one of the main reasons that people never start a business is that they procrastinate. Don't be that person.

**Final words on entrepreneurship, the great equalizer**

We are living in a great time and at a pivotal point in the history of entrepreneurship in this country. Now, it is easier and less expensive to start a business and become an entrepreneur. For many entrepreneurs, including myself, starting a business more than ten years ago meant that you had to have a physical address, maintain a printed calendar, remind yourself of meetings, and work primarily on a personal computer.

Today, you have access to all of these things in one device: a mobile phone. You have more apps that can help you increase efficiency and productivity than have been available at any time in history. How are you taking advantage of the opportunities and resources that you have in front of you? How are you positioning yourself to become an entrepreneur and create a legacy for your family? How do you take advantage of the opportunities at your disposal to help create stronger communities?

If you look at prosperous communities and cultures in America, they all have one key thing in common: a vibrant entrepreneurial culture. None of the successful communities in this nation are successful without a base of successful individual entrepreneurs and business owners. This is not to say that people who work jobs and have careers do not contribute to the economic success of their communities. But it does say that the longevity and stability of a community is dependent upon its ability to not only maintain the status quo, but to also grow the economic base.

In general, jobs alone are not enough to grow an economic base within a community. What grows an economic base is the exponential potential of a small business to perpetually create jobs and opportunities. It is my belief that if we are to empower our communities financially, we must focus on entrepreneurship – and that's entrepreneurship at all levels. That includes the guys on the corner washing cars and the hairdressers in the salons. Each needs to grow and develop his or her business in the same fashion that an entrepreneur in the tech industry would. They should be deliberate and methodical about it, too.

Entrepreneurship also helps to level the playing field in this country. If you want to go out and start a business tomorrow, depending on what that business is, you could do it. If you wanted to start a business that did not have specific regulatory requirements, you could do that today. If you wanted to start a business selling any sort of legal product or service, you could. As long as you could find the money to purchase the initial supplies or inventory needed to start your business, you could do that – and no one could stop you. In fact, if you started an online business, the initial investment would be even lower.

The only thing stopping you from becoming an entrepreneur is whatever limitations you put on yourself. So, what are you waiting for? Why aren't you living your dream? Why aren't you creating a legacy for your family? Why are you procrastinating?

Now is your time. Go ahead. Step out. Start up. Sustain.

Go ahead and say, "I Am the First!"